Gibbs'
Book of Architecture

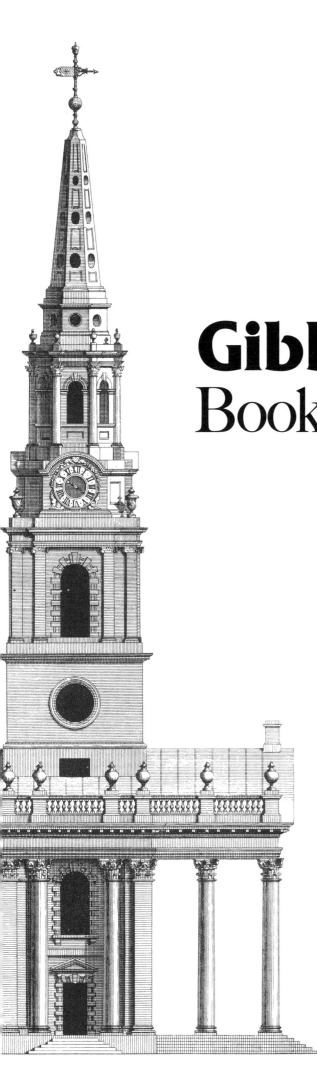

Gibbs'
Book of Architecture
AN EIGHTEENTH-CENTURY CLASSIC

DOVER PUBLICATIONS, INC.
MINEOLA, NEW YORK

Bibliographical Note

This Dover edition, first published in 2008, is an unabridged republication of the work originally published in London in 1728 under the title *A Book of Architecture, Containing Designs of Buildings and Ornaments*. Several of the plates have been slightly reduced to better accommodate the trim size.

Library of Congress Cataloging-in-Publication Data

Gibbs, James, 1682–1754.
    [Book of architecture, containing designs of buildings and ornaments]
    Gibbs' book of architecture : an eighteenth-century classic / James Gibbs.
        p. cm.
    Originally published under title: A book of architecture, containing designs of buildings and ornaments: London : W. Innys and R. Manby, J. and P. Knapton, and C. Hitch, 1728.
    ISBN-13: 978-0-486-46601-9
    ISBN-10: 0-486-46601-9
    1. Architecture—England—18th century—Designs and plans. 2. Decoration and ornament, Architectural—England—History—18th century—Designs and plans. I. Title. II. Title: Book of architecture.

NA966.G53 2008
720—dc22

2007052646

Manufactured in the United States of America
Dover Publications, Inc., 31 East 2nd Street, Mineola, N.Y. 11501

TO HIS GRACE

JOHN

Duke of *Argyll* and *Greenwich*, &c.

One of his MAJESTY's moſt Honourable Privy Council, Colonel of the
QUEEN's own Royal Regiment of
Horſe, General of the Foot, Ma-
ſter General of the Ordnance, and
Knight of the moſt Noble Order
of the Garter.

My LORD,

THE early Encouragement I received
from Your Grace, in my Profeſſion,
upon my Return from *Italy*, and the Honour
of

DEDICATION.

of Your Protection ever fince, give Your Name a juft Title to all my Productions in this kind.

AS feveral of the Defigns here exhibited have had Your Grace's Approbation; fo Your Patronage will be a fufficient Recommendation to the whole Work.

IT is a particular Pleafure to me that this Publication gives me an Opportunity to declare the real Sentiments of Gratitude and Refpect with which I am,

My *LORD,*

Your GRACE's

Moft Dutiful and moft

Obliged humble Servant,

JAMES GIBBS.

INTRODUCTION.

WHAT is here prefented to the Publick was undertaken at the inftance of feveral Perfons of Quality and others; and fome Plates were added to what was at firft intended, by the particular direction of Perfons of great Diftinction, for whofe Commands I have the higheft regard. They were of opinion, that fuch a Work as this would be of ufe to fuch Gentlemen as might be concerned in Building, efpecially in the remote parts of the Country, where little or no affiftance for Defigns can be procured. Such may be here furnifhed with Draughts of ufeful and convenient Buildings and proper Ornaments; which may be executed by any Workman who underftands Lines, either as here Defign'd, or with fome Alteration, which may be eafily made by a perfon of Judgment; without which a Variation in Draughts, once well digefted, frequently proves a Detriment to the Building, as well as a Difparagement to the perfon that gives them. I mention this to caution Gentlemen from fuffering any material Change to be

made

made in their Defigns, by the Forwardnefs of unskil-
ful Workmen, or the Caprice of ignorant, affuming
Pretenders.

SOME, for want of better Helps, have unfortunately
put into the hands of common workmen, the ma-
nagement of Buildings of confiderable expence; which
when finifhed, they have had the mortification to
find condemned by perfons of Taft, to that degree
that fometimes they have been pull'd down, at leaft al-
ter'd at a greater charge than would have procur'd better advice from an able Artift; or if they have ftood, they
have remained lafting Monuments of the Ignorance or
Parfimonioufnefs of the Owners, or (it may be) of a
wrong-judged Profufenefs.

WHAT heaps of Stone, and even Marble, are daily
feen in Monuments, Chimneys, and other Ornamental
pieces of Architecture, without the leaft Symmetry or
Order ? When the fame or fewer Materials, under the
conduct of a skilful Surveyor, would, in lefs room
and with much lefs charge, have been equally (if not
more) ufeful, and by Juftnefs of Proportion have had
a more grand Appearance, and confequently have better anfwered the Intention of the Expence. For it is
not the Bulk of a Fabrick, the Richnefs and Quantity
of the Materials, the Multiplicity of Lines, nor the
Gaudinefs of the Finifhing, that give the Grace or Beauty

ty and Grandeur to a Building; but the Proportion of the Parts to one another and to the Whole, whether entirely plain, or enriched with a few Ornaments properly difpofed.

In order to prevent the Abufes and Abfurdities above hinted at, I have taken the utmoft care that thefe Defigns fhould be done in the beft Taft I could form upon the Inftructions of the greateft Mafters in *Italy*, as well as my own Obfervations upon the antient Buildings there, during many Years application to thefe Studies: For a curfory View of thofe Auguft Remains can no more qualify the Spectator, or Admirer, than the Air of the Country can infpire him with the knowledge of Architecture.

If this Book prove ufeful in fome degree anfwerable to the Zeal of my Friends in encouraging and promoting the Publication of it, I fhall not think my Time mif-fpent, nor my Pains ill beftow'd.

I fhall now proceed to give a fhort Explanation of the Plates as they ftand in the Book.

THE Church of St. *Martin* in the Fields, *Weſtminſter*, being much decayed and in danger of falling, the Pariſhioners obtain'd an Act of Parliament for Rebuilding it at their own charges. The Commiſſioners appointed therein were pleaſed to make choice of me for Surveyor of that Work; and ſeveral Plans of different Forms being prepar'd and laid before them, they fix'd upon the following, as moſt proper for that Site. There were two Deſigns made for a Round Church, which were approved by the Commiſſioners, but were laid aſide upon account of the expenſiveneſs of executing them; tho' they were more capacious and convenient than what they pitch'd upon: I have inſerted them likewiſe in this Book. The Commiſſioners having ſign'd the Plan agreed on, gave me orders to begin the Work; and every thing being ready for laying the Foundation, His Majeſty was pleaſed to direct the Right Reverend the Biſhop of *Saliſbury*, then Lord Almoner, attended by Sir *Thomas Hewyt*, then Surveyor General, to lay the firſt Stone of this Fabrick; upon which was fix'd the following Inſcription:

D. S.

SERENISSIMUS REX GEORGIUS
PER DEPUTATUM SUUM
REV^{dum} ADMODUM IN X^{to} PATREM
RICHARDUM EPISCOP. SARISBUR.
SUMMUM SUUM ELEEMOSYNARIUM
ADSISTENTE (REGIS JUSSU)
D^{no} THO. HEWYT EQU. AUR.
ÆDIFICIORUM REGIORUM CURATORE PRINCIPALI
PRIMUM HUJUS ECCLESIÆ LAPIDEM
POSUIT
MARTII XIX° AN^o Dⁿⁱ MDCXXI
ANNOQUE REGNI SUI VIII^{vo}

This Ceremony being over, I proceeded with the Building, and fi-niſhed it in five Years; which, notwithſtanding the great Oeconomy of the Commiſſioners, coſt the Pariſh upwards of 32,000 Pounds. I have given here ſeven Plates of this Church.

P L A T E I.

A Perſpective View of it, taken from the South-Weſt Corner, ſhewing the South Side and Weſt Front, with the Steeple.

P L A T E

The new Church in the *Strand,* called St. *Mary le Strand,* was the firft publick Building I was employed in after my arrival from *Italy*; which being fituated in a very publick place, the Commiffioners for building the Fifty Churches (of which this is one) fpar'd no coft to beautify it. It confifts of two Orders, in the upper of which the Lights are placed; the Wall of the lower, being folid to keep out Noifes from the Street, is adorned with Niches. I have given fix Plates of it.

Plate XXI.

A Perſpective of the whole Building, ſhewing the South and Weſt Fronts with the Steeple. There was at firſt no Steeple deſign'd for that Church, only a ſmall *Campanile*, or Turret for a Bell, was to have been over the Weſt End of it: But at the diſtance of 80 feet from the Weſt Front there was a Column, 250 feet high, intended to be erected in Honour of Queen A n n e, on the top of which her Statue was to be placed. My Deſign for the Column was approved by the Commiſſioners, and a great quantity of Stone was brought to the place for laying the Foundation of it; but the thoughts of erecting that Monument being laid aſide upon the Queen's Death, I was ordered to erect a Steeple inſtead of the *Campanile* firſt propos'd. The Building being then advanced 20 feet above-ground, and therefore admitting of no alteration from Eaſt to Weſt, which was only 14 feet, I was obliged to ſpread it from South to North, which makes the Plan oblong, which otherwiſe ſhould have been ſquare. I have given two Plates of another Deſign I made for this Church, more capacious than that now built: But as it exceeded the dimenſions of the Ground allowed by Act of Parliament for that Building, it was laid aſide by the Commiſſioners.

Plate XXII.

The Under and Upper Plans of the Two different Orders of the ſecond Deſign.

Plate XXIII.

The Weſt End.

Marybone Chapell was built at the charges of the Right Honourable the Earl and Counteſs of *Oxford*, for the Accommodation of the Inhabitants of the new Buildings in *Marybone* Fields. It is a plain Brick Building, except the Portico, Coines, Door-caſes and the *Venetian* Window. The Cieling is handſomely adorned with Fret-work by Signori *Artari* and *Bagutti*.

Plate XXIV.

The North Side, with the Plan in ſmall.

Plate XXV.

The Weft Front, and the Section from South to North.

The Church of *Allhallows* in *Derby* is a very large Fabrick, join'd to a fine Gothick Steeple. It is the more beautiful for having no Galleries, which, as well as Pews, clog up and fpoil the Infide of Churches, and take away from that right Proportion which they otherwife would have, and are only juftifiable as they are neceffary. The plainnefs of this Building makes it lefs expenfive, and renders it more fuitable to the old Steeple. I have given two Plates of it.

Plate XXVI.

The South Side, and the Plan in fmall.

Plate XXVII.

The Eaft End and Section.

Plate XXVIII.

The Steeple of St. *Clement Danes*, which is built upon an old Foundation, at the charges of the Parifhioners. That part which is fhaded is the new Addition, and that in Lines is the Weft End of the Church, and the Veftry. The Plan of the Steeple is added on this Plate.

Plate XXIX, XXX.

Thefe two Plates contain Six of many more Draughts of Steeples made for St. *Martin*'s Church, with their Plans.

Plate XXXI.

Five Draughts of Steeples made for St. *Mary le Strand*, with their Plans. Steeples are indeed of a Gothick Extraction; but they have their Beauties, when their Parts are well difpos'd, and when the Plans of the feveral Degrees and Orders of which they are compos'd gradually diminifh, and pafs from one Form to another without confufion, and when every Part has the appearance of a proper Bearing.

Plate

King's College at *Cambridge* is now building by order of the Reverend Dr. *Snape*, Provoft of that College, and of the Fellows thereof. The Provoft, then Vice-Chancellor, laid the Firft Stone of this Fabrick. It is built of *Portland* Stone, and is detach'd from the Chapell as being a different kind of Building, and alfo to prevent damage by any accident of Fire. The Court could not be larger than is exprefs'd in the Plan, becaufe I found, upon meafuring the Ground, that the South-Eaft Corner of the intended Eaft Side of the Building came upon *Trumpington-Street*. This College, as defign'd, will confift of Four Sides, (*viz*) The Chapell, a beautiful Building of the Gothick Taft, but the fineft I ever faw; oppofite to which is propos'd the Hall, with a Portico. On one fide of the Hall is to be the Provoft's Lodge, with proper Apartments: On the other fide are the Buttry, Kitchin and Cellars, with Rooms over them for Servitors. In the Weft Side, fronting the River, now built, are 24 Apartments, each confifting of three Rooms and a vaulted Cellar. The Eaft Side is to contain the like number of Apartments.

PLATE XXXII.

The General Plan of the new Building, with the Chapell.

PLATE XXXIII.

The Weft Side fronting the River, and the Front of the Hall.

PLATE XXXIV.

The middle part of the Weft Side, upon a larger Scale.

PLATE XXXV.

The Sections of the Hall, which is 40 feet wide, 80 feet long and 40 feet high, to be finifh'd in Stucco.

PLATE XXXVI.

The Publick Building at *Cambridge*, of which I have given but one Plate; the Front in Perfpective, and the Plan in fmall over it. It confifts of a Library, the Confiftory, Regifter-Office and Senate-Houfe. The latter is already built with *Portland* Stone, as the reft of the Building is to be. It is of the *Corinthian* Order having all its Members enrich'd; the Cieling and Infide-Walls are beautify'd by Signori *Artari* and *Bagutti*.

PLATE

PLATE XXXVII.

The Plan and the two Fronts of a Houfe defign'd for a Perfon of Quality in *Somerfetfhire.* It is 143 feet in Front and 102 in the End-Fronts. You rife by ten Steps into a Hall of 30 feet by 40 and 20 feet high; and right forward there is a Cube-Room of 30 feet, which has on each fide a handfome Apartment 18 feet high. On each fide the Hall there is a Parlour and a Paffage of Communication to a Stone Stair-cafe: The firft Landing of which gives accefs to Interfoles over the Clofets, and the fecond to the upper Rooms. The Parlour on the right leads to the Chapell, and that on the left to two other Rooms. The Fronts are to be of rough Stone finifh'd with Stucco, but the Ornaments of the Windows, Doors, Coines, Cornifhes and other Proje6tions, of an excellent Stone dug near the place. The principal Front commands a fine Profpe6t of the *Severne,* and the Garden-Front a beautiful view of the Park.

PLATE XXXVIII.

A Draught made for *William Hanbury,* Efq; for a Houfe now building in *Northamptonfhire.* You rife four Steps and enter a Lobby of 13 by 18 feet, and thence pafs into a Room of 25 feet by 22, and 22 feet high, which has at each end a Room of 25 by 20 feet. On each fide the Lobby there is a Stair-cafe, and off of the Stairs a Room of 16 by 20 feet: Over this there are two Stories of Lodging Rooms, and under it convenient Offices all arch'd, and on each fide of the Court the Kitchin and Stables. The Front extends 84 feet by 46, and is to be built of Brick and the Ornaments of Stone.

PLATE XXXIX.

The Plan and Upright of the Right Honourable the Earl of *Litchfield*'s Houfe at *Ditchley* in *Oxfordfhire.* Here are ten Rooms on a Floor, befides two great Stairs and four Back-Stairs. You afcend ten Steps and enter a Hall of 31 feet 6 inches by 35 feet 2 inches, and 34 feet high, enrich'd with Fret-work and Painting. From the Hall you go into a Dining-Room towards the Garden of 23 feet by 31 feet 6 inches, which has a handfome Apartment upon the right hand, and on the left a Withdrawing-Room and a large Room of 36 feet by 21, with a Clofet and Back-Stairs. On each fide of the Hall there is a good Apartment,

partment, as likewife great Stairs, that lead up to the Chamber-Floor, and over that an Attick Story. The Kitchin-Offices are on one fide of the Houfe, and the Stables on the other, join'd by circular cover'd Paffages to the Houfe. The Houfe and Offices are built with an excellent Stone dug in that neighbourhood.

<h3 align="center">P<small>LATE</small> XL.</h3>

A *Villa* built for his Grace the Duke of *Argyll* at *Sudbrooke* near *Richmond* in *Surrey*, joining to *New-Park*. Here is a Cube-Room of 30 feet, handfomely adorn'd and lighted from two Portico's. It has two Apartments off of it, and over them Lodging Rooms. There are Vaults and other Offices under-ground. This Houfe is built of Brick, except the Ornaments, which are of *Portland* Stone.

<h3 align="center">P<small>LATE</small> XLI.</h3>

The Plan and two Fronts of a large Houfe for a Gentleman in the County of *York*, 230 feet in Front and 130 feet in the End-Fronts. You rife 10 feet by an eafy afcent to the principal Floor and enter a Hall 36 feet fquare, having an Apartment on each hand, and a Paf-fage 8 feet wide, that gives a Communication between the Great Stairs and Back-Stairs. Right forward from the Hall there is a Salon of 36 feet by 60, and 36 feet high, lighted from Courts 36 feet fquare, and beyond the Salon a Gallery 102 feet in length and 25 in breadth, with an Apartment at each end. In the middle of each End-Front there is a large Room, one for a Chapell and the other for a Library. This Story is 20 feet high, and underneath are convenient Offices 10 feet high, and over the grand Apartments good Lodging Rooms 15 feet high, cov'd $\frac{1}{3}$, with a convenient Paffage of Communication to ren-der all the Rooms private. This Building is of the Corinthian Or-der, rais'd on a Ruftick Bafement.

<h3 align="center">P<small>LATE</small> XLII.</h3>

The Plan and Upright of a Houfe 100 feet in Front and 70 feet deep. Here is a Hall of 30 feet by 32, and 15 feet high; and on each hand of it is a Room of 20 feet by 22, off of which there is a Clofet, and a Paffage that gives a Communication to the Offices. Straight forward from the Hall is a Dining-Room of the fame dimenfions with it, having on one fide a Withdrawing-Room, and a Bedchamber

on

on the other. There are two Stair-Cafes leading up to two Rooms of the fame dimenfions with the Hall and Salon, but double the height, cov'd and adorn'd with Fret-work. On each fide of thefe Rooms are alcov'd Bedchambers, and over them four other Apartments.

Plate XLIII.

A Draught of a Houfe made for a Gentleman in 1720. The Front is 71 feet by 54 in depth. Here is an Octagon Hall, on the right hand of which there is a Parlour and on the left the great Stairs. Right forward from the Hall there is a Dining-Room of 28 feet by 25, having a Withdrawing-Room and Back-Stairs on one fide and a Library on the other. This Story is 14 feet high, and the Rooms over them are 18 feet, and cov'd. The Fronts are uncommon, but have a good effect.

Plate XLIV.

The Plan, Front and Section of a Houfe made for a Gentleman in the fame Year, being 91 feet fquare. You afcend to a Portico of the Corinthian Order by 12 Steps, and enter a Hall of 22 feet by 33 and 20 feet high, and right forward an Octagon Salon of 33 feet and 40 feet high, lighted by Semicircular Windows as exprefs'd in the Section. Beyond the Salon is a Withdrawing Room of the fame dimenfions with the Hall. At each end of the Hall and Withdrawing-Room there are Rooms 22 feet fquare, with Clofets 10 feet 6 inches by 15 feet, and Interfoles over them. The Octagon Room may be private or publick at pleafure, becaufe of the Paffages of Communication betwixt the Hall and Withdrawing-Room. The Bedchambers over this Floor are alfo render'd very convenient by Paffages, which are lighted by round Openings in the Freeze of the great Room.

Plate XLV.

The Plan, Front and Section of a Houfe defign'd for a Gentleman in the Country. The Front is 36 by 95 feet deep. You rife by 12 Steps to a Portico, and then enter a Hall of 30 feet by 22, and go ftraight forward into a Salon of 55 feet by 33 and 40 feet high, lighted from above by 16 Windows; the Sides of the Salon are adorn'd with Pilafters, Niches, Figures and other Ornaments. From it you pafs into a Withdrawing-Room towards the Garden, of the fame dimenfions with the Hall. There are four noble Apartments on this Floor, each confifting of an Antichamber, Bedchamber and Clofet, and Inter-foles over the Clofets. All the Rooms on this Floor (except the Sa-lon and Clofets) are 20 feet high. There are two Stone Stair-cafes that lead to the upper Apartments which are 11 feet high; and are render'd private by Paffages of Communication between the Stair-cafes (exprefs'd by the prick'd Lines upon the Plan) which are lighted from the Freeze of the Salon.

Plate XLVI.

A Houfe intended to have been built at *Greenwich* in 1720. on a beautiful Situation. It is 130 feet in front by 90 feet deep, rais'd 5 feet above the level of a Court of 150 by 186 feet. You afcend 10 Steps to a Portico, and then enter a Salon of 35 by 30 feet, and 30 feet high; on each Side of which there is a very handfome Apart-ment. From the Salon you pafs forward to a Gallery of 25 by 76 feet, at each end of which there is an Apartment. There are great Stairs on each fide of the Salon, and a large Room of 22 by 25 feet in the middle of the End-Fronts: The Rooms on the principal Floor are 18 feet high, and the Lodging Rooms over them 13 feet. This Houfe was propos'd to have been built with *Portland* Stone, and finifh'd in a very expenfive manner.

Plate XLVII.

The two Fronts of the foregoing Plan, of the Ionick Order.

Plate XLVIII.

The Plan of a Houfe made for the Right Honourable Earl *Fitz-williams* to be built at *Milton* near *Peterborough*. It is 144 feet in front by 105 feet in depth, and confifts of 12 Rooms on a Floor, be-fides four Clofets, two Great Stair-cafes and four Back Stair-cafes: Here is a large Salon in Front, a Dining-Room towards the Garden and four noble Apartments, befides a Chapell and a large Billiard-Room. You either enter the Houfe upon the Level of the Court, or afcend from the Court to the principal Floor by Outfide-Stairs; and from the Garden in the fame manner. I have given two Plans of the Houfe on this Plate; the principal Floor, which is 15 feet high, and that of the Offices underneath.   Plate

Plate XLIX.

The Garden-Front of the foregoing Defign, and the Section of it from the Fore-Front to the Back-Front; fhewing the finifhing of the Salon, and of the reft of the Rooms within the line of this Section.

Plate L.

Another Draught which I made for the fame noble Lord, without the projecting Clofets and Stairs. It is 168 feet in front by 75 feet in depth, and has the fame number of Rooms and Conveniencies as the other, only varied in form and order.

Plate LI.

The Front of the laft Plan towards the Court, being of the Ionick Order, raifed on a Ruftick Bafement 15 feet high.

Plate LII.

A Draught made for *Edward Rolt*, Efq; for a Houfe intended to have been built in *Seacomb-Park* in *Hertfordfhire*; but the Execution of it was prevented by his Death. It is 136 feet in front and 72 feet deep. You afcend by 14 Steps to a Hall of 21 by 31 feet, and from thence enter a double Cube 30 feet wide, 30 feet high, and 60 feet long. It has four good Apartments, and publick Rooms in the middle of each End-Front. The upper Plan fhews the Lodging Rooms one pair of Stairs, which are all made private by a common Paffage between the Stairs.

Plate LIII.

The Front of the foregoing Plan, of the Ionick Order, rais'd on a Ruftick Bafement, with a regular Entablature round the whole Building. The Ornaments of the Outer Doors and Windows, the Columns, Entablature, Coines and Bafement, were propos'd to be of Portland Stone, and the reft of Brick.

Plate LIV.

The Plan and Front of a Defign made for a Perfon of Quality in 1720. From the Hall you enter between a double Stair-cafe into a Dining-Room richly adorn'd, having a handfome Apartment on each Hand. The Stairs are lighted from above.
Plate

Plate LV.

A Draught made for *Matthew Prior*, Efq; to have been built at *Down-Hall* in *Effex*. It is 63 ½ feet in front by 43 ½ feet in depth. From a Court of 90 feet by 78 you afcend three Steps and enter through an arch'd Portico into a Hall 25 feet fquare, which leads into a Parlour and Withdrawing-Room on one hand, and a Library on the other, with Great and Back-Stairs. The Room over the Hall is a Cube of 25 feet, and has a Bedchamber and Clofet on one fide, and two Rooms, each 16 feet fquare, on the other, as mark'd by prick'd Lines. The Cube-Room is lighted on two fides from two Portico's of the Dorick Order. The Offices are on each fide of the Court, having a cover'd Communication from the Houfe by an Arcade. Mr. *Prior*'s Death prevented the building of this Houfe.

Plate LVI.

A Draught made for a Gentleman in *Wiltfhire*. It contains fix Rooms on a Floor, befides four Clofets and two Stair-cafes. The Offices are on each fide of the Court, which is of an Octagonal form. The Fronts are of Brick. The Coines, Ornaments of the Windows, Fafcia's and Cornifh are of Stone.

Plate LVII.

A Houfe Defign'd for a Gentleman in the Country, extending 101 feet in front by 64 in depth. You rife 8 Steps from a Court 160 feet fquare, and enter a Hall of 25 feet by 35, and pafs forward into a Gallery 70 feet long and 22 feet wide, having Clofets at each end. The Gallery may be divided into three Rooms upon occafion. On each fide of the Hall there are Rooms of 20 by 22 feet, and Clofets, with Paffages to the Offices, and two Stair-cafes that lead up to fix Rooms and eight Clofets one pair of Stairs, and to the fame number of Rooms over them. The principal Floor is 16 feet high, the fecond 14, and the upper 8.

Plate LVIII.

A Defign made for a Gentleman in *Dorfetfhire*. It is 77 feet in front and 44 feet deep, having fix Rooms on a Floor, with Clofets and two Stair-cafes. The Offices are on each fide of an Octagonal Court.

Plate LIX.

A Defign made for the Right Honourable the Earl of *Ilay* for his *Villa* at *Whitton* near *Hampton-Court*. It is 82 feet in front by 56 in depth. From a Portico of 30 feet by 10 you enter a Room of 30 feet by 40, and 30 feet high; on each fide of which there is an Apartment. This Building is of the Ionick Order. The Portico, Windows, Fafcia's, Entablature, and all the projecting parts were propos'd to be of Stone, and the reft of Brick finifh'd over with Stucco.

Plate LX.

The Plan of the fecond Floor, and a Section of the foregoing De-fign. There are four Bedchambers, two Clofets and two Stair-cafes on this Plan. The great Room goes two Stories high, as is exprefs'd by the Section; by which the height of the other Rooms are likewife fhown.

Plate LXI.

Two Plans and a Front of a little Houfe propos'd to my Lord *Ilay* for the fame place. Out of a Porch you enter a Room of 20 feet by 40 and 20 feet high; beyond which there are two Rooms of 14 feet by 18 ¦ and 9 ¦ feet in height, with a Stair-cafe betwixt them that leads to Rooms over them of the fame dimenfions. Upon the 2 pair of Stairs Floor and over the large Room are 4 Rooms 10 feet high. The lower Plan fhews the under-ground Story. The Kitchin is in a Court at one end of the Houfe, and the Servants Hall at the other, with a Paffage of Communication through the Houfe. The Chimneys of the Kitchin and Servants Hall are carried into the Wall of the Houfe, and the Roof of them is skreen'd by a Wall 10 feet high. Befides three Vaults under the great Room, there are Rooms below for the Houfekeeper and other Conveniencies. The Fronts are propofed to be of Brick, plaifter'd over, and all the projecting parts to be of Stone.

Plate LXII.

Another Defign for *Whitton*, 72 feet in front by 43. I have given two Plans and a Front of it upon this Plate. You afcend five Steps into a Portico, and thence go into an arch'd Salon of 20 feet by 40, and 25 feet high, lighted from the Fore and Back-Fronts, by Semi-

circular

circular Lights, and two Windows one on each fide of the Door. There are four Rooms with Clofets off of the Salon, and four more over them, with two Stair-cafes. The Offices under-ground are manag'd as in the foregoing Draught; as alfo the Kitchin and Servants Hall, which are in Courts without-doors.

Plate LXIII.

A Houfe of 58 by 44 feet, containing fix Rooms on a Floor, with two Stair-cafes. The Kitchin is on one fide of the Court, and the Stables on the other, with Rooms over them, and are join'd to the Houfe by circular Arcades. The Rooms on the principal Floor are 12 feet high. The Front is plain, with Architraves round the Windows. The Defign was made for a Gentleman in *Torkfhire*.

Plate LXIV.

A Draught done for a Gentleman in *Effex*. I have given on this Plate the general Plan of it, and two Fronts. From a Court of 115 feet by 93, the Angles fweeping off, you afcend by five Steps into a Hall of 28 feet by 22, and pafs forward to a Dining-Room of 18 feet by 28 towards the Garden, having on the right a Withdrawing-Room, a Bedchamber and Dreffing Room, and on the left a Waiting Room and a Library of 30 feet by 18. The Body of the Houfe is only 73 feet by 47, the Bedchamber and Clofet on one fide, and the Library on the other, going only one Story high. The Rooms on the principal Floor are 16 feet high, and the Chamber Story over them is 12 feet high. On each fide of the Hall, there is a Stair-cafe, and alfo a Room out of which you go through a Dorick Colonnade to the Offices on each fide of the Court.

Plate LXV.

The Plan and Front of a Houfe of fix Rooms on a Floor with two Stair-cafes, made for a Gentleman in *Oxfordfhire*. The principal Rooms are 16 feet high, and the Chamber Story 11.

Plate LXVI.

A Defign of a Houfe for a fingle Gentleman, 61 feet in front and 33 feet deep. The Hall is 14 feet 6 inches by 24 feet, in which is the Stair-cafe. Beyond that is a Dining-Room of 24 feet by 18, having

two

two Rooms at each end. On the next Floor there are feven fmall Lodging Rooms, all private. The Ornaments of the Fronts are of Stone, and the reft of Brick.

Plate LXVII.

The Plan, Upright and Section of a Building of the Dorick Order in form of a Temple, made for a Perfon of Quality, and propos'd to have been placed in the Center of four Walks; fo that a Portico might front each Walk. Here is a large Octagonal Room of 22 feet and 26 feet high, adorn'd with Niches and crown'd with a Cupola. All the Ornaments of the Infide are to be of Plaifter, and the Outfide of Stone.

Plate LXVIII.

A Defign of a Building for the Right Honourable the Earl of *Oxford*'s Bowling-Green at *Down-Hall* in *Effex*. I have here given two Plans, a Front and Section of it; that on the right hand is the Ground-Plan; the Middle part to be open, for fhelter in cafe of Rain, having a Clofet on one fide, and a Stair-cafe on the other. Over this Plan is the Front: The Ruftick Arcade, Coines, Niches, Venetian Windows, and Modillion-Cornifh to be of Stone. The Plan upon the left fhews the Story one pair of Stairs, wherein there is a Room of 27 feet by 20, and 25 feet high, having a Clofet, or little Withdrawing-Room, within it of 10 by 20 feet. There are two Venetian Windows to the great Room, and one at each end of the Building which light the Clofet and the Stair-cafe.

Plate LXIX.

Two other Pavillions propos'd for the fame place; the one is an Octagon Room of 30 feet, with a Clofet on one fide, and on the other a Stair-cafe, which leads to the Waiting Rooms underneath. The other is a Cube of 25 feet, having a Waiting Room on one fide, and a Clofet on the other. The Fronts of both were to be plain Brick-work; the Cornifh, Window-cafes and Door-cafes to be of Stone.

Plate LXX.

A Pavillion defign'd for Sir *John Curzon* for his Seat near *Derby*. It is a Cube of 20 feet, adorn'd with three Venetian Windows, circular

cular Niches for Bufto's, and an Entablature fupported by Ruftick Coines. There were two of them to have been built oppofite to one another, on each fide of a Vifta propofed to be cut through a Wood, and to be terminated with an Obelifque upon a Hill fronting the Houfe; the execution of which was prevented by Sir *John's* Death.

PLATE LXXI.

The Plan, Upright and Section of a Room built by the Honourable *James Johnston* Efq; at *Twickenham*, being 30 feet over, and 34 feet high, richly adorn'd by *Artari* and *Bagutti* with Fret-Work, and the proper Ornaments gilt. It is built with Brick and Stone.

PLATE LXXII.

A circular Building in form of a Temple, 20 feet in Diameter, having a Periftylium round it of the Dorick Order, and adorn'd with a Cupola; erected in his Grace the Duke of *Bolton's* Garden at *Hackwood*, upon the upper ground of an Amphitheatre, back'd with high Trees that render the Profpect of the Building very agreeable.

PLATE LXXIII.

Two Uprights of another Pavillion built at *Hackwood*. The Ruftick Front looks upon a fine piece of Water, and the other on a beautiful Parterre.

PLATE LXXIV.

The Plan and Section of the foregoing Pavillion.

PLATE LXXV.

The Plan, Upright and Section of a Pavillion for the Right Honourable the Lord Vifcount *Cobham* in his Garden at *Stow* in *Buckinghamfhire*.

PLATE LXXVI.

Another Defign for two Pavillions at *Stow*; both built of Stone in the fame form without; but within the one is an Octagon Room of 24 feet, the other is divided into Rooms, and made a Dwellinghoufe for a Gentleman.

Plates LXXVII, LXXVIII.

Eight fquare Pavillions for my Lord *Cobham* and others.

Plate LXXIX.

Four Summer-houfes in form of Temples, Defign'd for feveral perfons.

Plate LXXX, LXXXI.

Eight more of an Octagon form.

Plate LXXXII.

Two Seats for the ends of Walks.

Plate LXXXIII.

Two other Seats for the fame purpofe.

Plate LXXXIV.

Two Draughts of a Building for the Menagery at *Hackwood*. The Portico of the one is with Arches, and the other with Columns; having a Room at each end, and two Rooms behind for the perfon that looks after the Pheafants. That with the Columns is built.

Plate LXXXV.

Three Draughts of Obelifques. The Antients have left us in the dark as to the Proportion of thefe Ornaments with refpect to their Height. Thofe at *Rome* being all different, there can be no Rule taken from them. I have in thefe Draughts fhewn three different Proportions for them; *viz.* 8, 7, and 6 times the bignefs at the Bottom to the Height. The firft (tho' neareft to that before St. *Peter*'s) appearing too high, and the laft too low, I fhould recommend the other, as a Medium between the two Extreams; as likewife the following Rules to be obferved in forming them; *viz.* The Obelifque to diminifh one Third, the Diamond Point to form a Rectangle, the Bafe to be in height half the thicknefs of the Bottom of the Obelifque, and the Bafe, Pedeftal and Plinth to be three times that Thicknefs.

PLATE

Plate LXXXVI.

Three Draughts of Obelifques, more ornamental than the former: They keep the fame Proportion with them; only that upon the left hand has four times the thicknefs of the Obelifque at bottom to the height of its Pedeftal, becaufe of the Ornaments upon it. The top-part may be made in the manner here drawn, or with other Ornaments at difcretion. The Antients never placed their Obelifques upon moulded Bafes; but *Dominico Fontana* and others have placed them upon Bafes, which, in my opinion, is a great addition to their beauty; however that may be done or not at pleafure.

Plate LXXXVII.

Three Defigns for Columns, proper for publick Places or private Gardens; *viz.* a plain Dorick Column upon its Pedeftal with a Vafe a-top, a fluted Column properly adorn'd, and a Ruftick frofted Column, with a Figure a-top, as I have made them for feveral Gentlemen. The Proportions of them are mark'd upon an upright Line, divided into fo many Diameters of the Column for the Height.

Plate LXXXVIII.

Six Draughts of Peers for Gates, and three Defigns of Iron-work betwixt them.

Plate LXXXIX.

Two other Defigns of Peers, with Iron-work.

Plate XC.

Two Defigns for Peers and Iron-work for large Courts.

Plate XCI.

Three Draughts of Chimney-pieces, with Ornaments over them for Pictures, done for feveral Gentlemen.

Plate XCII.

Three Defigns of Chimneys done for Meff. *Clark* and *Young* at *Rowhampton.*

Plate

an

an excellent Sculptor.   Mr. *Prior's* Busto was done at *Paris* by M. *Coizivaux*, Sculptor to the King of *France.*

Plate CXIII.

A Monument now making to the Memory of *Edward Colston*, Esq; to be erected at *Bristol.*   The Figures are by Mr. *Ryfbrack.*

Plate CXIV.

A Monument erected at *Bolsover* in *Derbyshire*, by the Right Honourable the Earl and Countess of *Oxford*, to the Memory of *Henry* Duke of *Newcastle*, and others of the *Cavendishe* Family buried there.

Plate CXV.

A Monument for Mrs. *Catharina Bovey*, placed in *Westminster-Abby.* The Figures are very well handled by Mr. *Ryfbrack.*

Plate CXVI.

A Design for a Monument for His Grace the late Duke of *Buckingham.*

Plate CXVII.

A Monument for a Gentleman in the Country.

Plate CXVIII.

A Monument for a Noble Lord and Lady, executed with some variation.

Plate CXIX.

A Design of a Monument for a Person of Quality.

Plate CXX.

A Monument erected in *Westminster-Abby* for the Right Honourable the Marchioness of *Annandale.*

Plate CXXI.

A Monument set up by *Montague-Gerrard Drake*, Esq; in the Church of *Agmondesham*, for his Father and Mother.

PLATE CXXII.

Three Monuments. The middlemoſt is Mr. *Smith*'s in *Weſtminſter-Abby*; the Figure and Medal done by Mr. *Ryſbrack*. The two others are done in the Country; the one for a Lady, the other for a Gentleman.

PLATE CXXIII.

Three Monuments: The middle one is Sir *John Bridgman*'s ſet up at *Aſhton* in *Warwickſhire*, and the others for two Ladies.

PLATE CXXIV.

Three Monuments: The middle one is *Ben. Johnſon*'s, erected at the charge of the Right Honourable the Earl of *Oxford*, in *Weſtminſter-Abby*; that upon the right was deſign'd for another Poet, and the other for Mr. *Wanley*, his Lordſhip's Librarian.

PLATE CXXV.

Three Monuments made for the Country.

PLATE CXXVI.

Three Monuments Deſign'd for ſeveral places.

PLATE CXXVII.

Three Monuments with Pyramids: The middle one is ſet up for *Robert Stuart*, Eſq; in St. *Margaret*'s Church, *Weſtminſter*.

PLATES CXXVIII, CXXIX.

Six Compartments for Monumental Inſcriptions, upon black Marble grounds.

PLATES CXXX, CXXXI, CXXXII.

Nine large Compartments for Inſcriptions, or Coats of Arms.

PLATES CXXXIII, CXXXIV, CXXXV.

Eighteen ſmall Compartments for Monumental Inſcriptions.

Plates **CXXXVI, CXXXVII.**

Sixteen Defigns for Sarcophagus's, or Monumental Urns, in the Antique Taft.

Plate **CXXXVIII.**

Three Defigns for Vafes, done for the Right Honourable the Earl of *Oxford.* There are two Vafes well executed in Portland Stone according to the middle Draught, which are fet upon two large Peers on each fide of the principal Walk in the Garden at *Wimpole* in *Cambridgefhire.*

Plates **CXXXIX, CXL, CXLI, CXLII, CXLIII, CXLIV.**

Fifty four Draughts of Vafes, *&c.* in the Antique manner, made for feveral perfons at different times. Many of them have been executed both in Marble and Metal.

Plate **CXLV.**

Eight Draughts of Marble Cifterns for Buffets.

Plate **CXLVI.**

Six other Cifterns rais'd upon Pedeftals, which may alfo ferve for Fonts.

Plate **CXLVII.**

Eight Defigns for Marble or Stone Tables, for Gardens or Summer-Houfes.

Plates **CXLVIII, CXLIX.**

Eighteen Defigns for Pedeftals of Dyals. In my Opinion it is much better for Gentlemen to have Pedeftals of this fort, than to have their Dyals fupported by Figures, unlefs they be very well executed: Thefe may be done by a common Workman, and are equally ufeful and lefs expenfive.

Plate **CL.**

Fifteen Pedeftals for Bufto's.

A LIST

A
LIST
OF THE
SUBSCRIBERS.

A.

DUKE of Argyll, &c.
Duke of Athol.
Earl of Abingdon.
Earl of Aberdeen.
Earl of Aylesford.
Alexander Abercrombie, Esq;
Mr. William Adams, Architect.
Mr. William Aikman.
James Anderson, M. A.
Mr. John Anderson, Merchant.
Mr. John Andrews.
Sir John Anstruther, Bart.
Col. Philip Anstruther.
Andrew Archer, Esq;
Thomas Archer, Esq;
Richard Arnold, Esq;
Mr. David Audsley.
Sir John Austen, Bart.
George Aylworth, Esq;

B.

DUKE of Beaufort.
Duke of Bolton.
Duke of Bedford.
Marquis of Blandford.
Lord Bolingbroke.
Lord Bathurst.
Lord Bingley.
Lord Byron.
Lord Binning.
Thomas-Sclater Bacon, Esq;
Sir Walter-Wagstaffe Bagot, Bart.
Mr. John Bagutty.
John Barber, Esq;
Mr. John Barnes.
Sir John Barrington, Bart.
Mr. John Basset.
Mr. John Bates.
Benjamin Bathurst, Esq;
Thomas Beake, Esq;
Mr. Daniel Bell.
Richard Bellasyse, Esq;
Mr. John Belshaw.
Mr.   Bennet, Carpenter.
Benjamin Benson, Esq;
Hon. Col. Henry Berkeley.
Hon. Henry Bertie, Esq;
Dr. John Betsworth.

Mr. Richard Billinghurst.
Mr. Francis Bird.
Stephen Bisse, Esq;
Major General Bisset.
Martin Bladen, Esq;
Mr. John Blake.
Mr. John Blow.
Charles Bodenham, Esq;
The Bodleyan Library.
Dennis Bond, Esq;
John Boulter, Esq;
George Bowes, Esq;
William Bowles, Esq;
Sir Roger Bradshaigh, Bart.
Orlando Bridgeman, Esq;
Mrs. Bridgeman of Hanover-Square.
Mr. Charles Bridgeman.
John Brinsden, Esq;
Robert Bristow, Esq;
Sir Charles Buck, Bart.
Alexander Burne, Esq;
Mr. Thomas Buss

C.

DUKE of Chandos.
Marquis of Carmarthen.
Earl of Cardigan.
Earl of Carlisle.
Earl of Coventry.
Lord Viscount Cobham.
Lord Viscount Chetwynd.
Lord Clinton.
Lord Craven.
Lord Colraine.
Baron Clark.
Charles Cæsar, Esq;
Hon. Col. James Campbell.
Col. John Campbell.
Sir William Carew, Bart.
Mr. Christopher Cass.
William Chetwynd, Esq;
Jerningham Cheveley, Esq;
Mr. John Christmass.
Mr. Thomas Churchill.
Mr. Robert Churchill.
Sir Thomas Clarges, Bart.
Bartholomew Clark, Esq;
Mr. Francis Cleare.
Mr. John Clements.
Robert Coatsworth, Esq;

Mr. Christopher Cock.
Henry Coghill, Esq;
Benjamin Collier, Esq;
John Conduit, Esq;
Sir George Cook.
George Cook, Esq;
Mr. William Cooper.
Sir John Cope, Bart.
Sir Robert Cornwall, Bart.
Col. Henry Cornwall.
Sir Clement Cotterell.
Mr. John Cotterell.
John Cotton, Esq;
Philip Craig, Esq;
Mr. John Craig of Glasgow.
Major General Crofts.
John Cross, Esq;
George Crowle, Esq;
John Crowley, Esq;
Sir John Curzon, Bart, deceased.

D.

DUKE of Devonshire, Lord President of the Council.
Duke of Dorset, Lord Steward of the Houshold.
Earl of Danby.
Earl of Dalkeith.
Earl of Dunmore.
Lord Delaware.
Lord Dupplin.
Lord Dun.
Mr. Michael Dahl.
Sir James Dalrymple, Bart.
George Dashwood, Esq;
Sir Jermyn Davers, Bart.
Mr. Isaac Daws.
Sir Matthew Decker, Bart.
Conrade de Gols, Esq;
Sir Edward Dering, Bart.
Mr. John Desborough.
Sir Edward Desbouvrie, Bart.
Ambrose Dickins, Esq;
Hon. Col. George Douglas.
Mr. John Dow.
Mountague-Gerard Drake, Esq;
Mr. William Draycott.
John Drummond, of Norfolk-street, Esq;
Mr. Andrew Drummond.

Nicholas

Nicholas Dubois *Esq;*
Mr. Francis Duck.
William Duffe, *Esq;*
Mr. Thomas Dun.
Anthony Duncombe, *Esq;*
Robert Dundafs, *Esq;*
Sir John Dutton, *Bart.*
Mr. George Duval.

E.

EARL of Effex.
Lord Erfkine.
Lord Effingham.
William Eaft, *Esq;*
Richard Edgcombe, *Esq;*
William Edgeworth, *Esq;*
Thomas Edwards, *Esq;*
Sir John Erfkine, *Bart.*
Mr. James Effex, *of* Cambridge.
Mr. William Etty, *of* York.
Sir John Eyles, *Bart.*
Sir Jofeph Eyles.
Mr. James Eyles.

F.

EARL of Findlater *and* Seafield.
Earl Fitzwilliams.
Lord Vifcount Falconberge.
Lord Foley.
Hon. Col. Fane.
Mr. Matthew Faulkner.
Coulfon Fellowes, *Esq;*
Hon. John Finch, *Esq;*
Richard Fleming, *Esq;*
Mr. Henry Flitcroft.
Mr. Auditor Foley.
Richard Foley, *Esq;*
William Forbes, *Esq;*
Hon. Theophilus Fortefcue, *Esq;*
Sir Andrew Fountaine.
Sir Thomas Frankland, *Bart,*
Ralph Freeman, *Esq;*
William Freeman, *Esq;*
Rev. Robert Freind, *D. D.*
John Freind, *M. D.*
William Fullerton, *M. D.*
Sir Robert Furnefe, *Bart.*

G.

DUKE of Grafton.
Earl Godolphin.
Lord Gower.
Lord Grange.
Thomas Gape, *Esq;*
Edward Gibbon, *Esq;*
Mr. Thomas Goff.
Mr. Jefharelah Golding.
Mr. Samuel Gooding.
Sir William Gordon, *Bart.*
William Gore, *Esq;*
Mr. Anthony Goud.
Sir Archibald Grant, *Bart.*
Mr. George Greaves.
Mr. David Gregory, *Profeffor of Modern Hiftory and Languages in Oxford.*
Mr. Thomas Griffin.
Mr. Charles Griffith.
Sir Richard Grofvenor, *Bart.*
Thomas Grofvenor, *Esq;*
John Gumley, *Esq;*

H.

DUKE of Hamilton, *&c.*
Earl of Hertford.
Earl of Huntington.
Earl of Haddingtoun.
Earl of Hopeton.
Earl of Hallifax.
Lady Margaret-Cavendifhe Harley.
Jofeph Hall, *Esq;*
Mr. John Hallam.
Charles Halfted, *Esq;*
Richard Hampden, *Esq;*
Newburg Hamilton, *Esq;*
William Hanbury, *Esq;*
Sir Thomas Hanmer, *Bart.*
Edward Harley, *Esq;*
Sir John Harper, *Bart.*
George Harrifon, *Esq;*
Mofes Hart, *Esq;*
Francis Hawes, *Esq;*
Philip Hawkins, *Esq;*
Nicholas Hawkfmoor, *Esq;*
Millington Hayford, *Esq;*
John Heidegger, *Esq;*
Anthony Henley, *Esq;*
John Herring, *Esq;*
Mr. Thomas Hinton.
Herman Hoburg, *Esq;*
Rev. Dr. Holdfworth.
Major Gen. Honywood.
Robert Honywood, *Esq;*
Mr. James Horne.
Col. Horfey.
Mr. Stephen Horfman.
John How, *Esq;*
Mr. John How, *Carver.*
Hugh Howard, *Esq;*
Mr. William Hubert.
Mr. John Hughes.
Orlando Humphreys, *Esq;*
Maurice Hunt, *Esq;*
Thomas Hunt, *Esq;*

I.

EARL of Ilay.
Lord Vifcount Irwin.
Theodore Jacobfon, *Esq;*
John James, *Esq;*
Mr. John James, *of Covent-Garden.*
Mr. Stephen Theodore Janffen.
Mr. William Jefferfon.
Mr. Andrew Jelfe.
Mrs. Anne Jennens.
Charles Jennens, *Esq;*
William Jennens, *Esq;*
Mr. John Jenner.
Ralph Jennifon, *Esq;*
Mr. William Iles.
Hon. James Johnfton, *Esq;*
Mr. Thomas Johnfon.
Charles Jones, *Esq;*
James Joye, *Esq;*
Henry Joynes, *Esq;*

K.

DUKE of Kent.
Earl of Kinnoull.
Henry Kelfal, *Esq;*
William Kent, *Esq;*
Mr. William King.
Col. Kirk.

Bulftrode Peachy Knight, *Esq;*
Mr. Thomas Kynafton.
Sir William Kyte, *Bart.*

L.

EARL of Lincoln.
Earl of Litchfield.
Earl of Lauderdale.
Earl of Lowdon.
Lord Lewifham.
Lord Lonfdale.
Sir John Lambert, *Bart.*
Mr. John Lane.
Mr. Leake, *Bookfeller at* Bath.
Sir Thomas Lee, *Bart.*
Mr. Walter Lee.
Right Rev. Dr. Leng, *late Bifhop of* Norwich, *deceafed.*
Smart Lethieullier, *Esq;*
Col. Ligoniere.
Edward Lifle, *Esq;*
Philip Lloyd, *Esq;*
William Lock, *Esq;*
Mr. John Lock.
Sir Thomas Lowther, *Bart.*
Mr. John Ludbey.
Mr. William Ludbey.

M.

DUKE of Montrofe.
Lord Morpeth.
Lord Malpas.
Lord Mafham.
Mr. Alexander Mac-Gill, *Architect.*
Mr. Richard Marples.
Mr. John Mackreth.
Buffy Manfel, *Esq;*
Mr. Ifaac Mansfield, *Sen.*
Mr. Ifaac Mansfield, *Jun.*
Thomas Mafters, *Esq;*
John Maunder, *Esq;*
Richard Mead, *M. D.*
Sir Philip Meadowes, *Bart.*
John Mearde, *Esq;*
Rev. Dr. Middleton.
Col. John Middleton.
Mr. George Middleton.
Carew Harvey Mildmay, *Esq;*
Charles Miller, *Esq;*
Mr. John Mift.
Dr. William Mitchel.
David Mitchel, *Esq;*
Sir Humphrey Monoux, *Bart.*
Mr. John Montigny.
Mr. John More.
Mr. Thomas More.
Sir William Morgan, *Knight of the Bath.*
John Morley, *Esq;*
Sir William Morrice, *Bart.*
Mr. Roger Morris.

N.

DUKE of Norfolk.
Earl of Northampton.
John Neale, *Esq;*
Mr. John Neale.
Mr. John Norris.

O.

EARL of Orkney.
Earl of Oxford.

Countefs

Countess of Oxford.
Crew Offley, Esq;
Mr. John Ogle.
Sir Adolphus Oughton, Bart.

P.

DUKE of Powys.
Earl of Pembroke.
Earl Poulet.
Lord Naffau Powlet.
Lord Parker.
Lord Peifley.
Lord Perfival.
Lord Palmerfton.
Henry Pacey, Esq;
Sir Gregory Page, Bart.
Thomas Palmer, Esq;
Humphrey Parfons, Esq;
Mr. James Pafcal.
Mr. Henry Pafmore.
Tho. Paterfon, Esq;
Charles Pelham, Esq;
Mr. Thomas Penley.
Philip Perfival, Esq;
Daniel Pettiward, Esq;
Richard Philips, Esq;
Mr. Thomas Phillips.
Mr. William Pickering.
Mr. William Porter.
Hon. Robert Price, Esq; One of the
    Juftices of the Court of Common
    Pleas.
Mr. John Prince.
Rt. Hon. William Pulteney, Esq;
Daniel Pulteney, Esq;
Col. Harry Pulteney.

Q.

DUKE of Queenfbury and Dover.
Queen's College Library at Ox-
    ford.

R.

DUKE of Richmond.
Duke of Roxburgh.
Earl of Rothes.
Mr. John Read.
Mr. Edward Reeves.
Mr. Thomas Reeves.
Mr. John Reynolds.
John Rich, Esq;
Mr. James Richards.
Thomas Ripley, Esq; Comptroller of
    his Majesty's Works.
John Roberts, Esq;
Thomas Robinfon, Esq;
George Rooke, Esq;
Lieut. Gen. Rofs.

Rev. Dr. Rundle.
Mr. Michael Ryfbrack.

S.

DUKE of Somerfet.
Earl of Scarfdale.
Earl of Stafford.
Earl of Scarbrough.
Earl of Stairs.
Earl of Strafford.
Earl of Suffex.
Lord St. John of Bletfhoe.
Lord Southwell.
Thomas Sadler, Esq;
Sir John St. Aubyn, Bart.
Sir Jeremiah Sambrooke, Bart.
Jeremiah Sambrooke, Esq;
John Sambrooke, Esq;
Mr. George Sampfon.
Sir Thomas Samuel, Bart.
Sir Thomas Saunderfon, Knight of
    the Bath.
Mr. Will. Sayer.
Mr. William Scarfe.
Thomas Scawen, Esq;
Gervafe Scroope, Esq;
Sir Thomas Saunders-Sebright, Bart.
Mr. Enoch Seeman.
Mr. John Senex.
Francis Seymour, Esq;
Mr. Tho. Shepard, Mafon.
Mr. John Shepard.
Samuel Shepherd, Esq;
Mr. John Shirley, of Durham.
Mr. Michael Sidnell.
Mr. William Simons, of Woodftock.
Sir Henry Slingfby, Bart.
Mr. John Smalwell.
Henry Smith, Esq;
Simon Smith, Esq;
Sir Edward Smyth, Bart.
Rev. Dr. Snape, Provoft of King's
    College, Cambridge.
William Sorefbey, Esq;
Mr. Robert Speckman.
Sir William Stapleton, Bart.
Sir John Stapylton, Bart.
Rev. William Stratford, D. D.
Dr. Alexander Stewart.
Sir William Strickland, Bart.
Mr. Edward Strong.
Col. James Stuart.
Mr. John Sturt.
Mr. Robert Style.
Robert Surman, Esq;
Mr. John Symmonds.

T.

LORD Vifcount Townfhend, Prin-
    cipal Secretary of State.
Earl of Thomond.

Lord Vifcount Tyrconnel.
John Talbot, Esq;
William Thomas, Esq;
Sir James Thornhill.
William Thornton, Esq;
Mr. Peter Tillemans.
Mr. Benjamin Timbrell.
William Tims, Esq;
John Tovey, Esq;
Hon. Thomas Townfhend, Esq;
Mr. William Townfend of Oxford.
William Tryon, Esq;
Edward Tucker, Esq;
Mr. Samuel Tuffnell.
Cholmondeley Turner, Esq;
Sir Halfwel Tynte, Bart.

V.

LORD Vane.
Sir Peter Vandepot, Bart.
Henry Vane, Esq;
Anthony Vanfittart, Esq;
Mr. Richard Vanfpangen.
Mr. George Vertue.
Robert Viner, Esq;

W.

EARL of Wymes.
Lord Waldgrave.
Right Hon. Sir Robert Walpole,
    Knight of the Garter, &c.
Thomas Walker, Esq;
John Ward, Esq;
Right Rev. Thomas, Lord Bifhop of
    Waterford.
William Wenman, Esq;
Hon. Sir Thomas Wentworth, Knight
    of the Bath.
Sir Anthony Weftcomb, Bart.
Mr. —— Wexham.
Sir John Williams, Bart.
Mr. Roger Williams.
Mr. Henry Williams.
Sir William Willip, Bart.
William Winde, Esq;
Charles Withers, Esq;
Mr. Leonard Wooddefon.
Mr. John Woodall.
Chriftopher Wren, Esq;
Mr. Robert Wren.
George Wright, Esq;
Thomas Wright, Esq;
Matthew Wymondefold, Esq;
Sir William Wyndham, Bart.
Watkin Williams Wynn, Esq;

Y.

Hitch Young, Esq;

The Plates

A Perspective View of S.t Martins Church

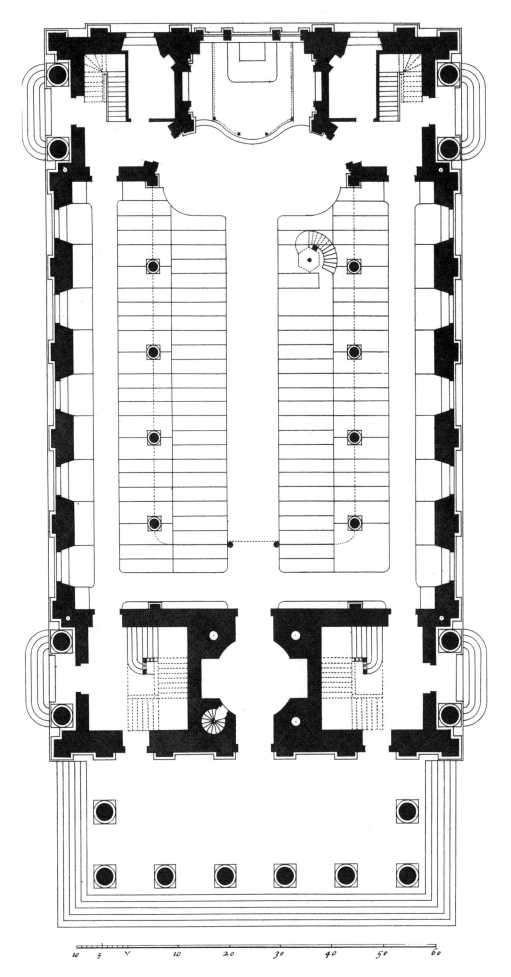

10 5 V 10 20 30 40 50 60

The Plan of the Church of St. Martin.

The West front of St Martins Church.

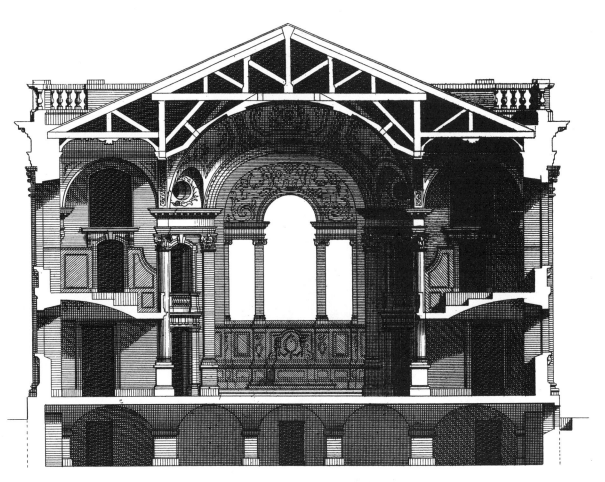

Section from South to North

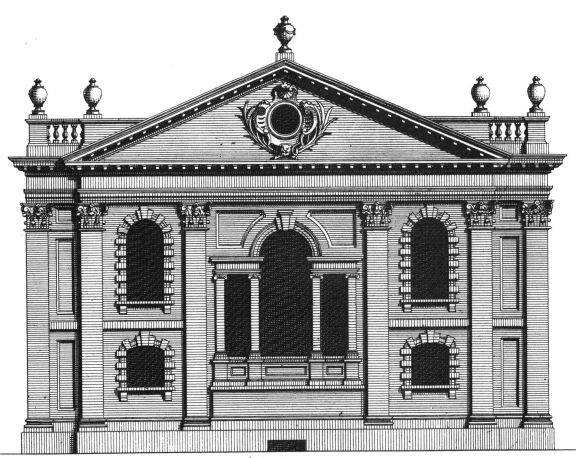

The East End

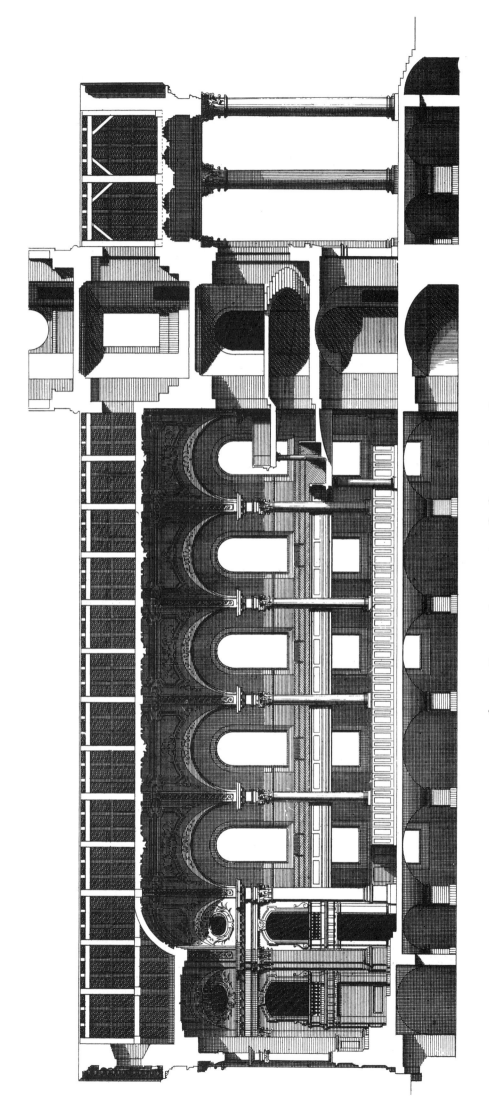

The Section from Eaſt to Weſt of St. Martins Church.

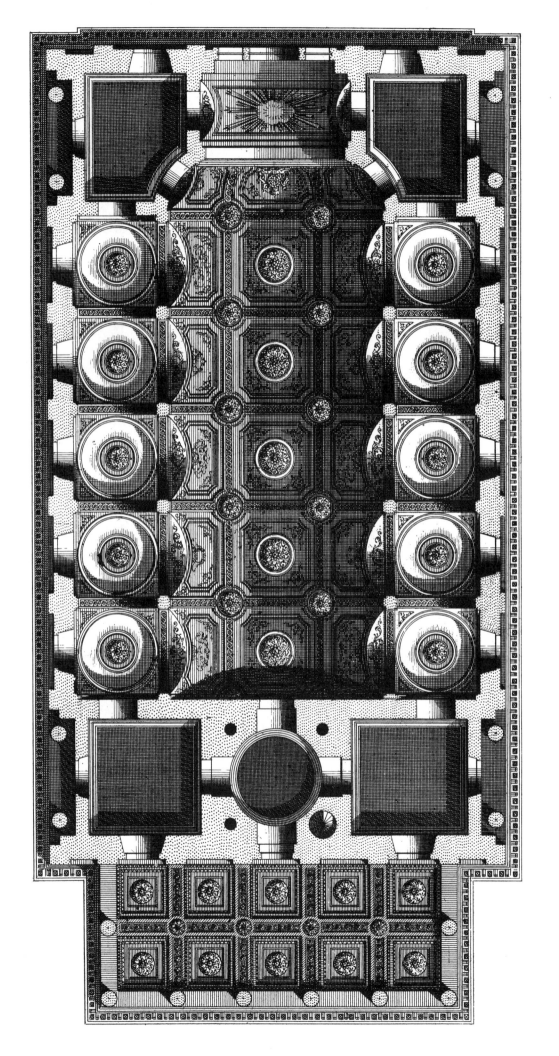

The Ceiling of the New Church of St Martin

The North Side of St. Martins Church.

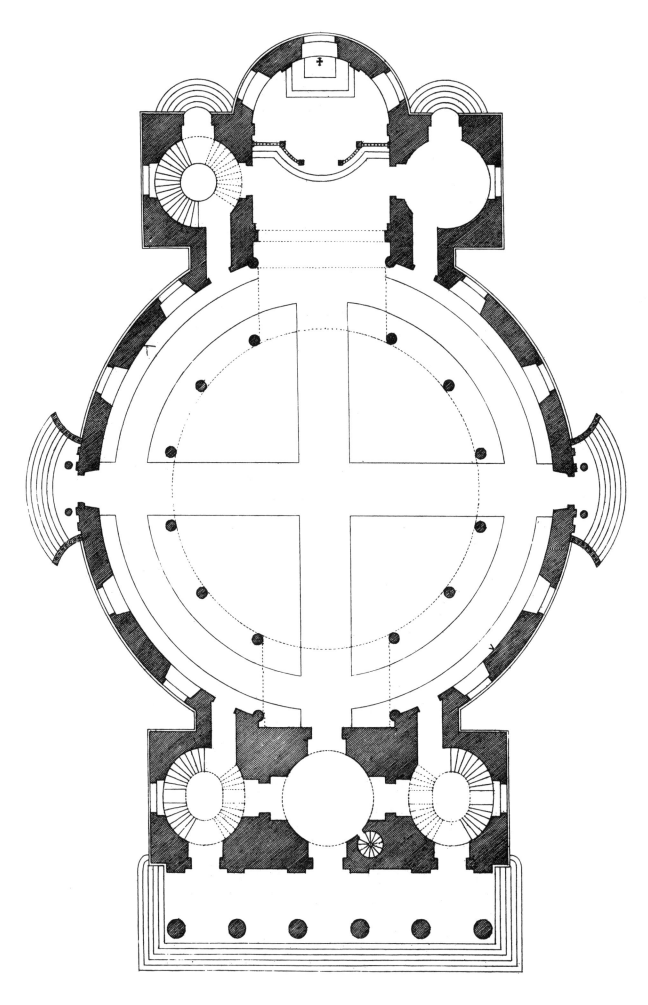

The West End.

The North Side .

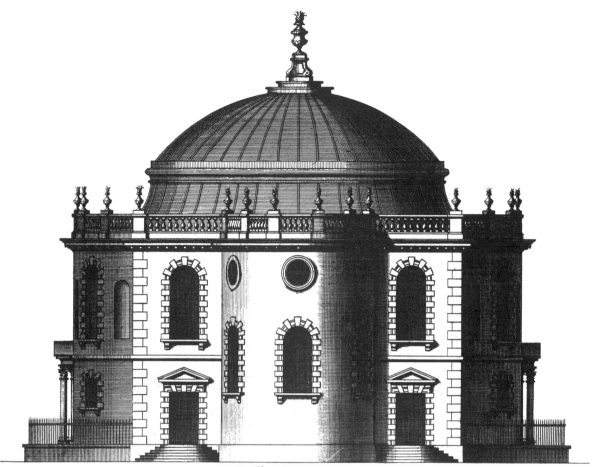

The East End

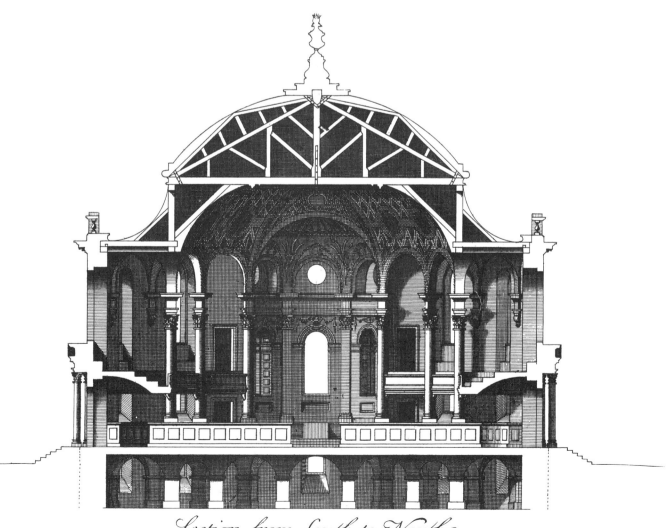

Section from South to North

The Section from East to West.

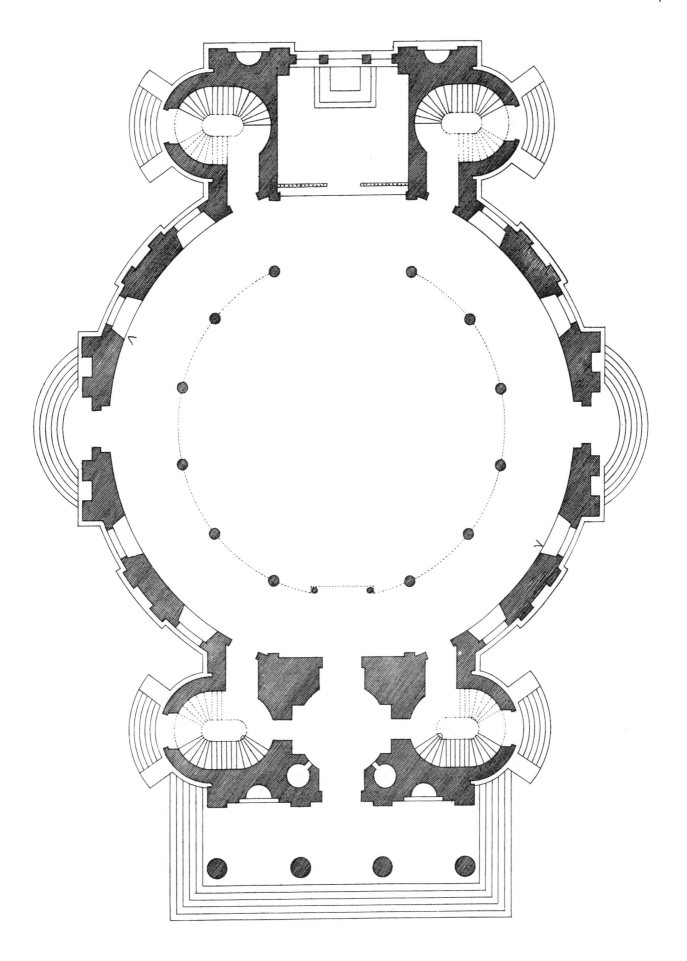

West End

South Side.

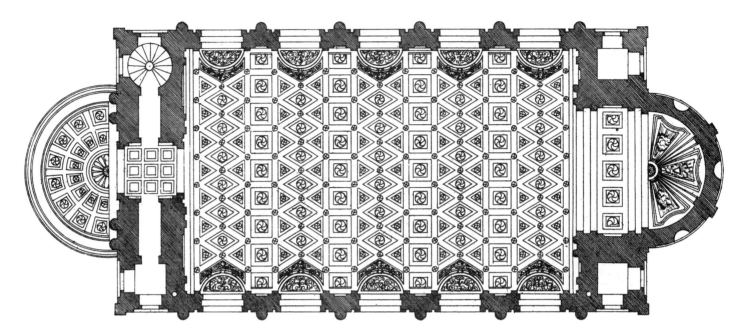

Plan of the Upper Order.

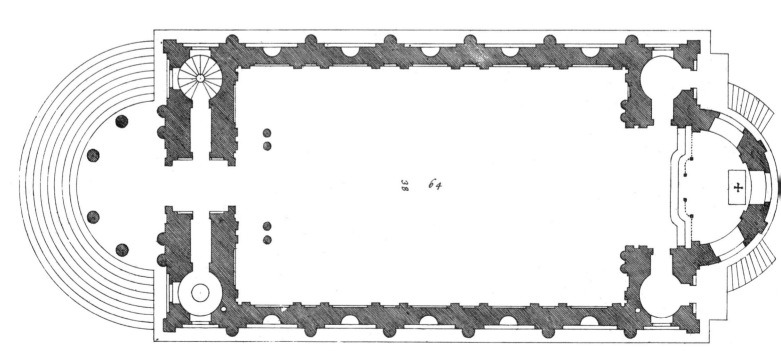

38   64

Plan of the Under Order.

The West-end

The East end

The South side.

Profpectũs Templi St.æ Mariæ Londini in vico dicto the Strand, Architectura Iacobi Gibbs.

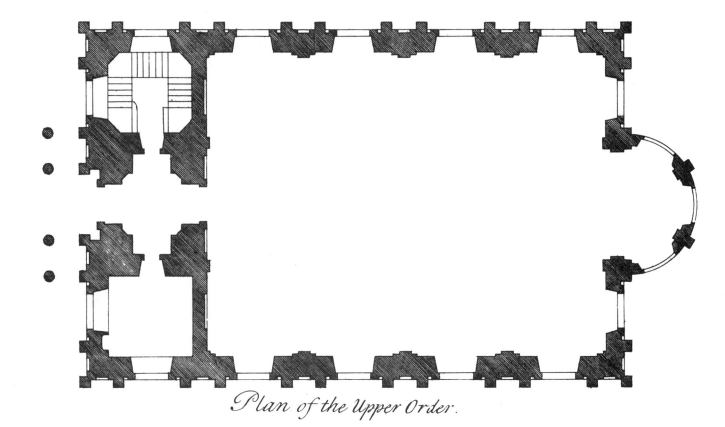

Plan of the Upper Order.

Plan of the under Order.

The West-end.

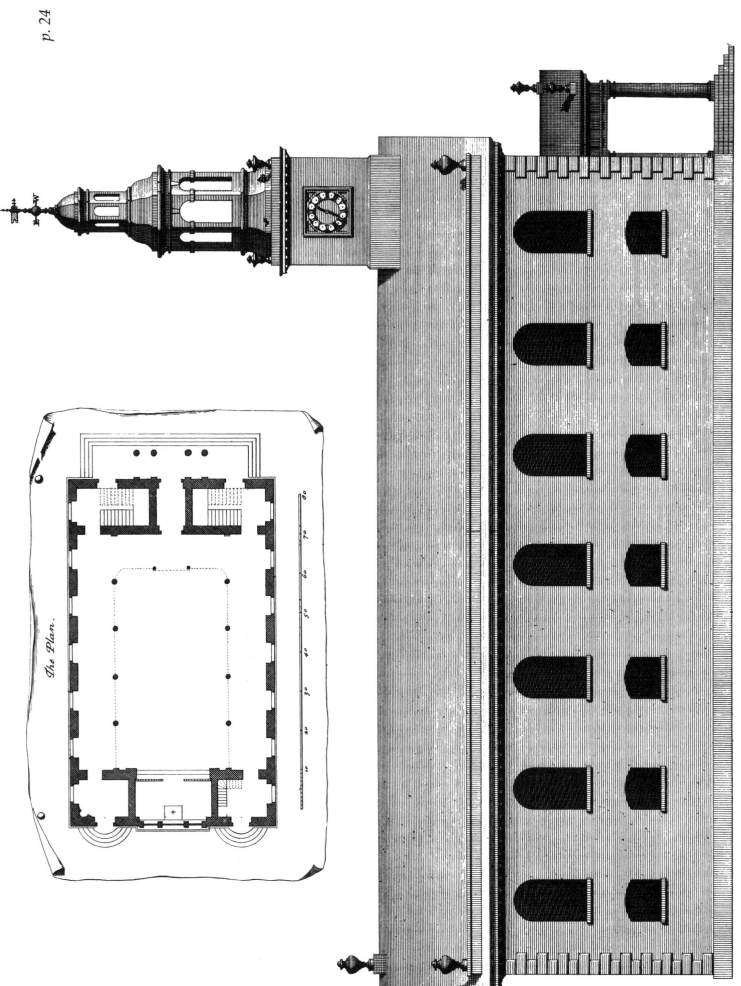

The Plan.

The North Side.

The West Front

The Section from South to North.

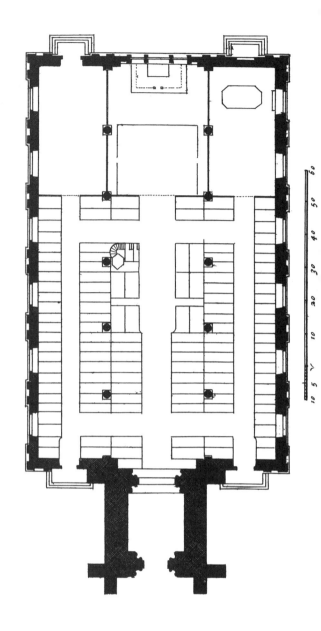

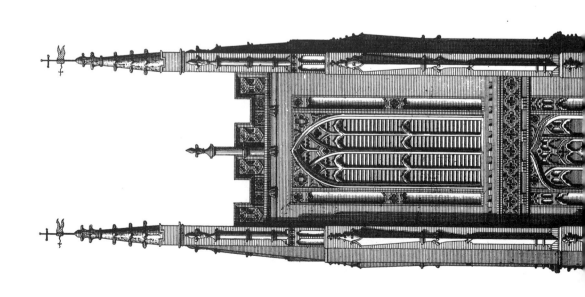

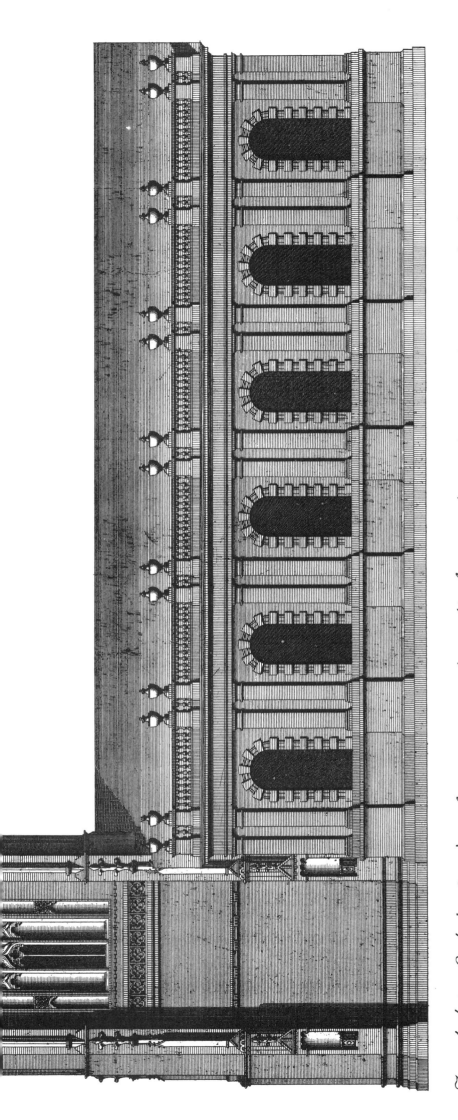

Australe latus Ecclesiæ Omnium Sanctorum, apud Derbienses, mox ab imis instaurandæ, una cum Sepulchrali Monumento, in quo Reliquiæ Prænobilis Devoniæ Prosapiæ conduntur, Stante adhuc Turri magnificâ, quæ ad 178 pedes caput sublime attollit, Minister & Paro" chiani ejusdem Ecclesiæ Duci Devoniensi, Viro non minus integris moribus, quam splendidis Natalitiis illustri, humillime dedicant.

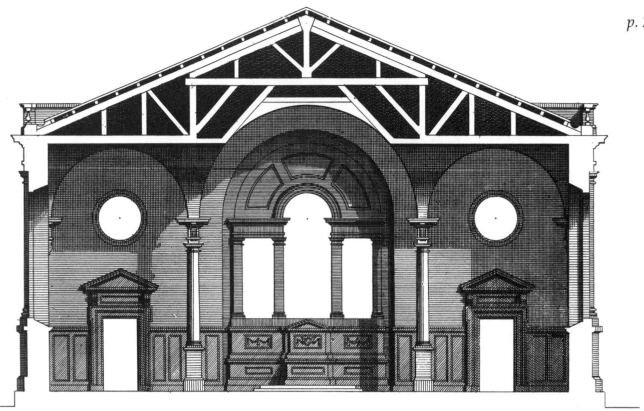

The Section.

The East end of the New Church att Derby.

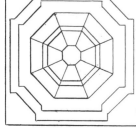
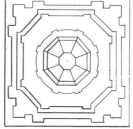
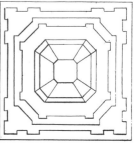

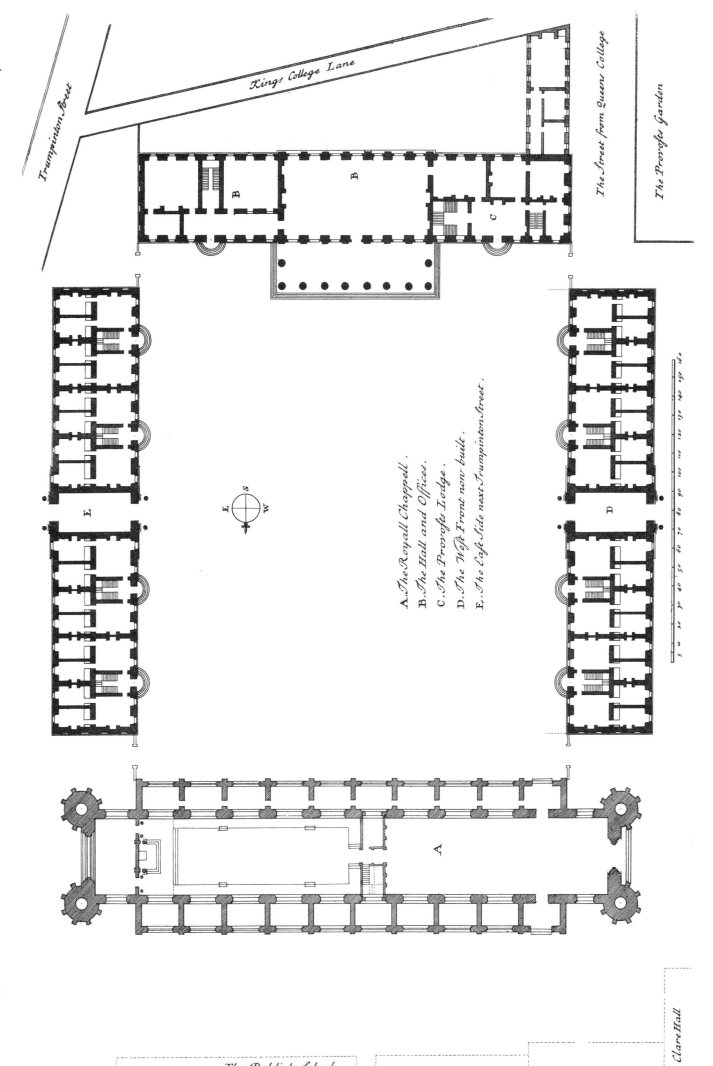

Trumpinton Street

Kings College Lane

The Street from Queens College

The Provosts Garden

B

B

C

E

D

A

S
E   W
N

A. The Royall Chappell.
B. The Hall and Offices.
C. The Provosts Lodge.
D. The West Front now built.
E. The East Side next Trumpinton Street.

5 10 20 30 40 50 60 70 80 90 100 110 120 130 140 150 160

The Publick Schools

Clare Hall

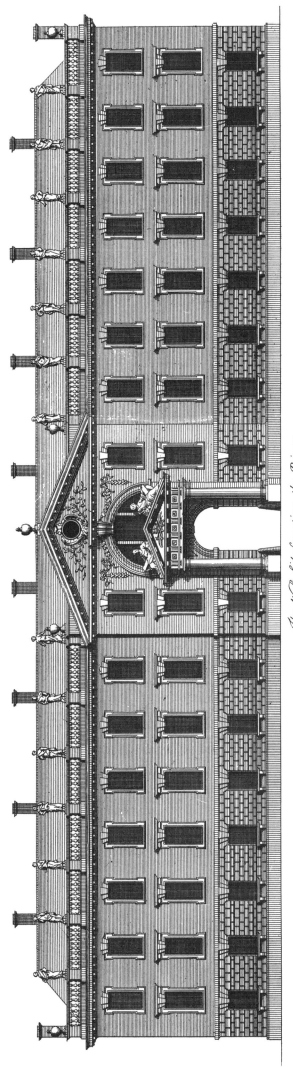

The West Side fronting the River.

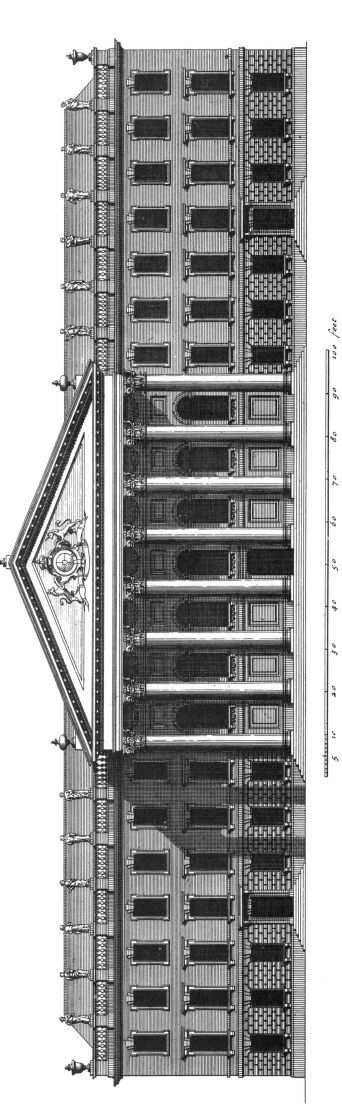

The upright of the South Side of Kings College fronting the Chapel.

5 10 20 30 40 50 60 70 80 90 100 feet

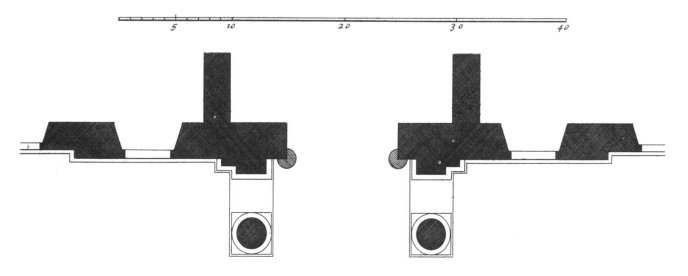

The middle parte of the West Side upon a larger Scale ——

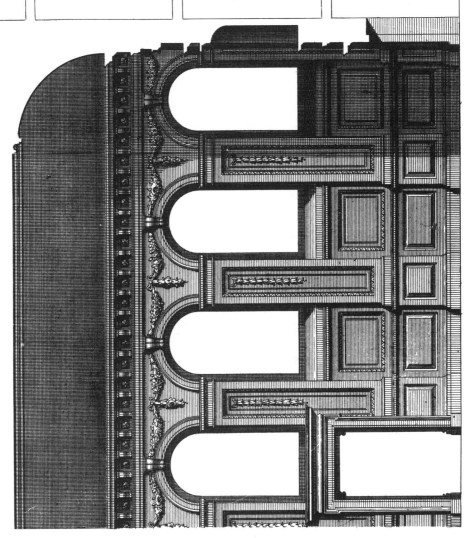

The halfe of the Section of the Hall of Kings College longwise.

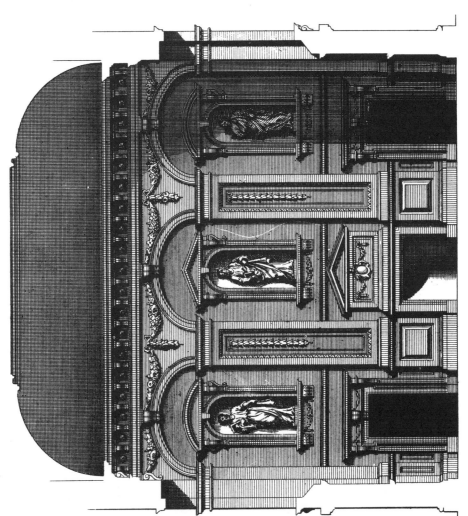

The Section for the end of the Hall.

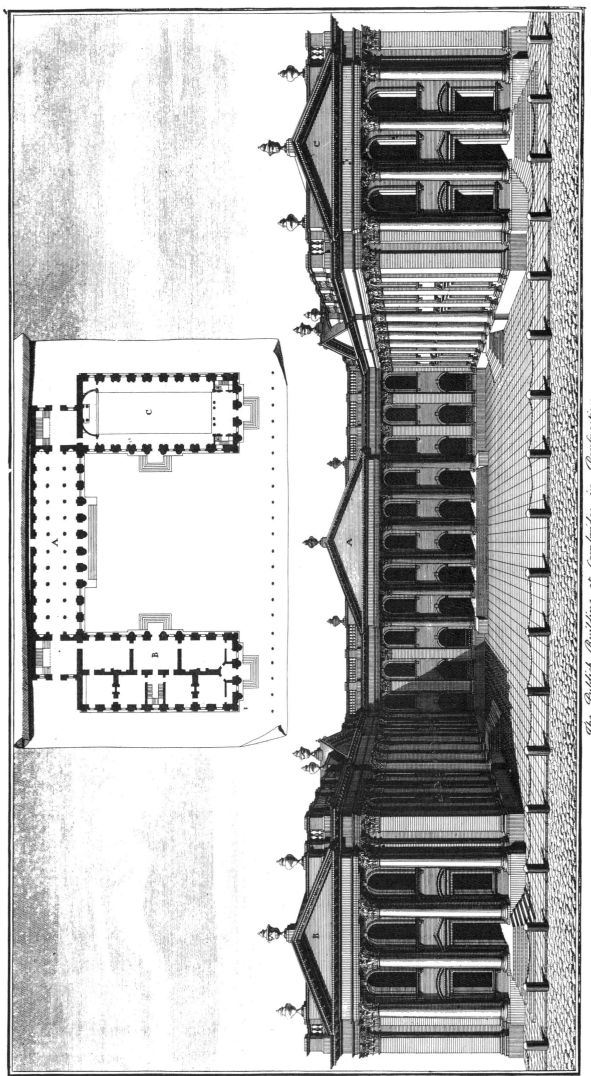

The Publick Building at Cambridge in Perspective

A The Royal Library
B The Confistory & Regifter Office
C The Senate Houfe

The Princepal Front towards the Court

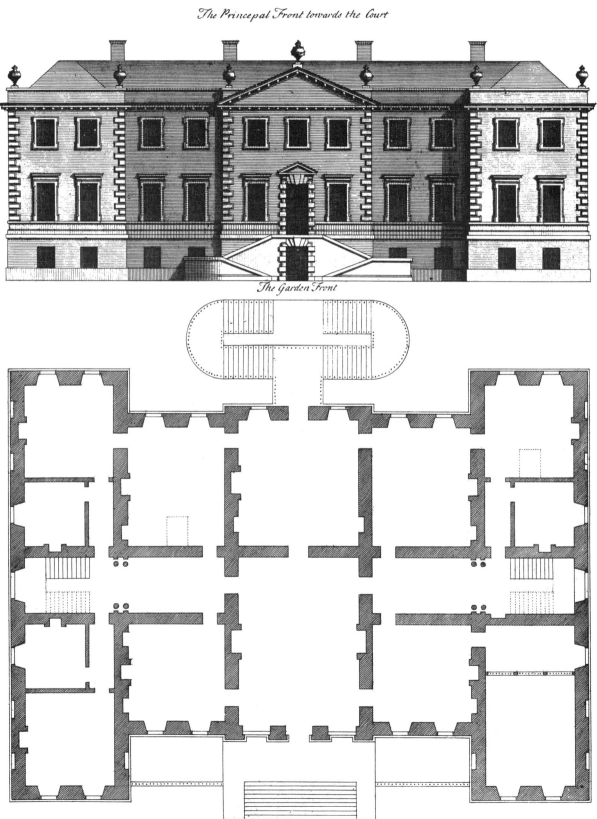

The Garden Front

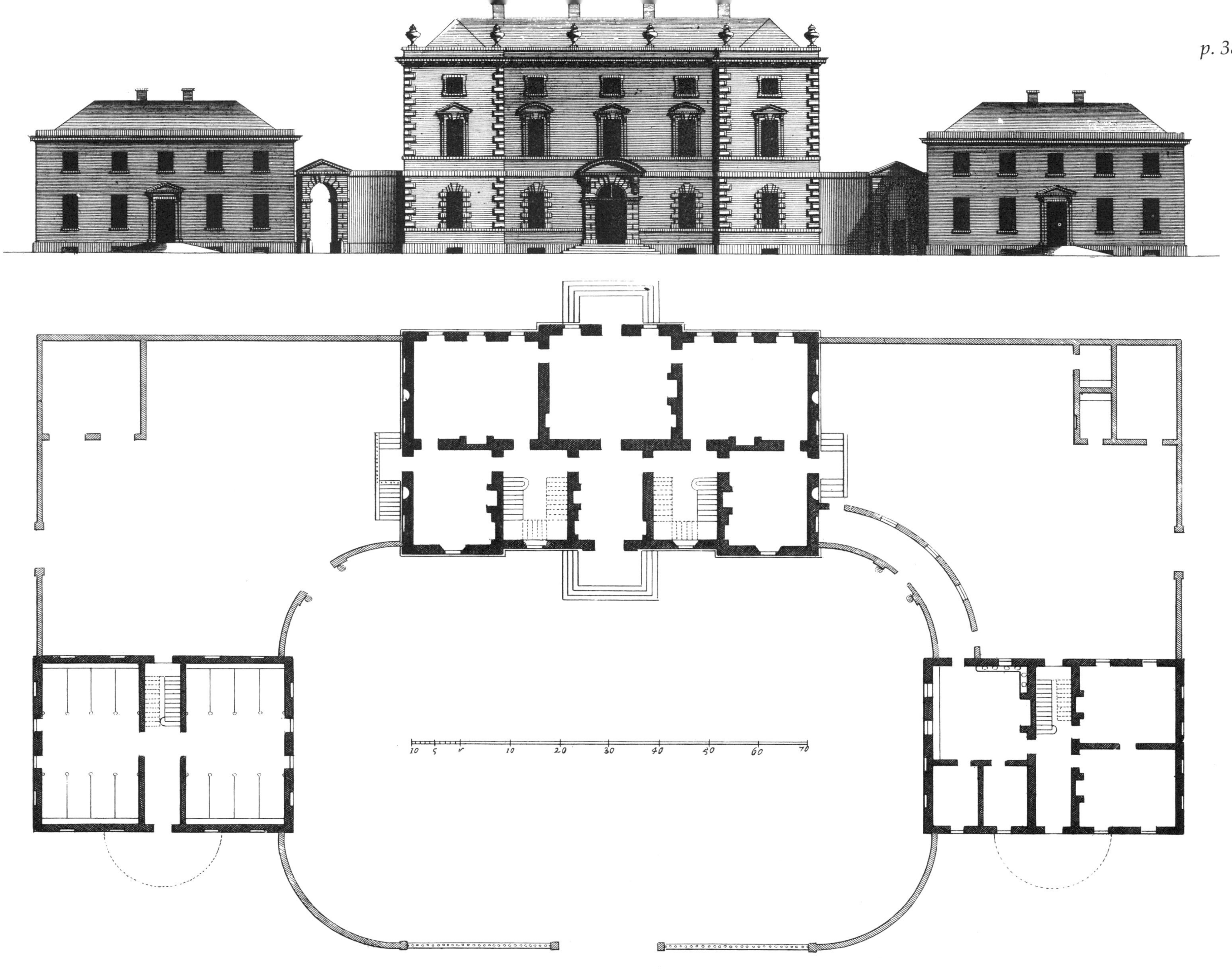

p. 38

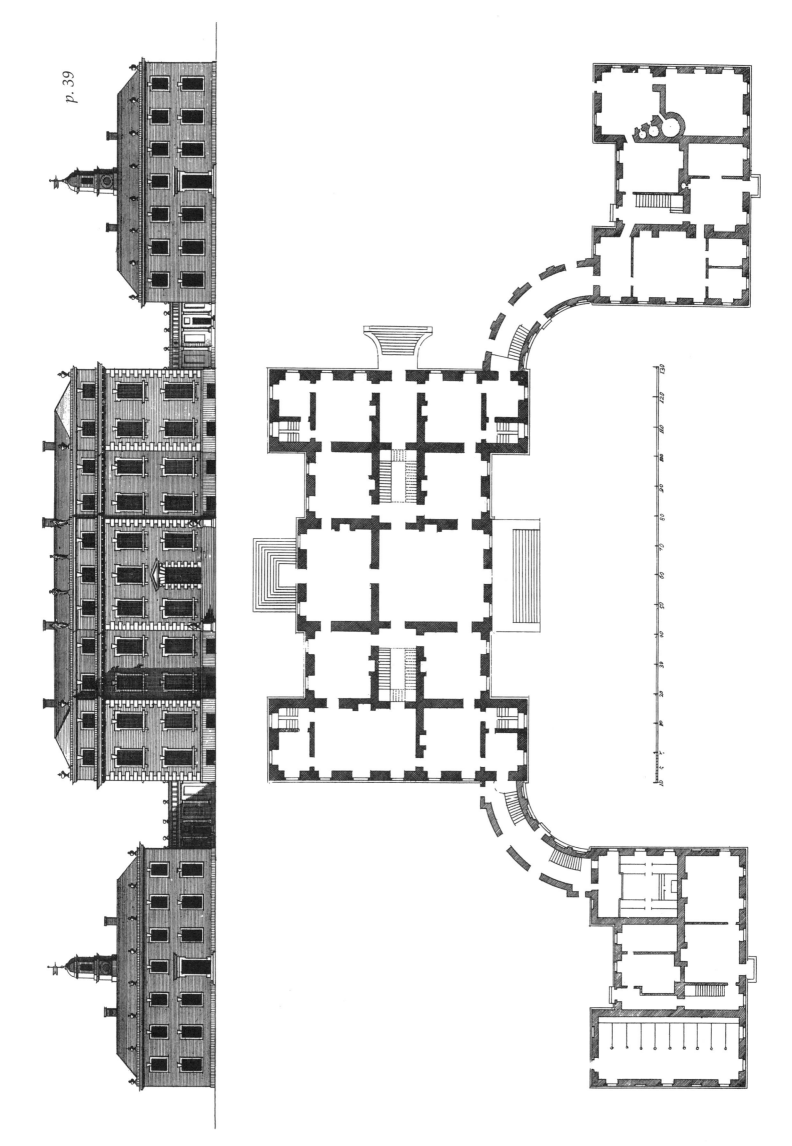

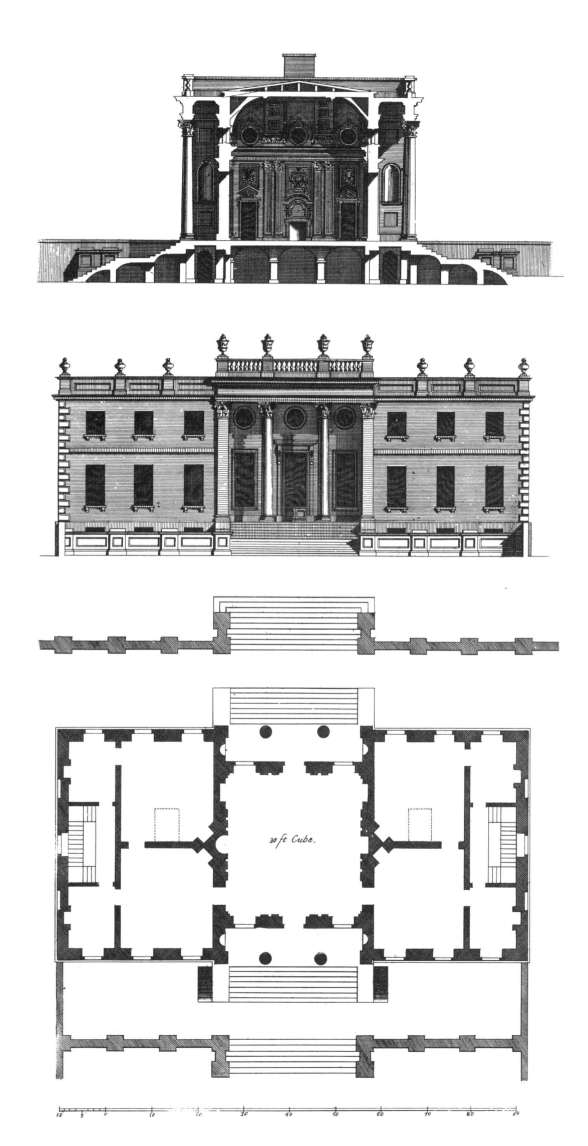

30 ft Cube.

Front towards the Garden

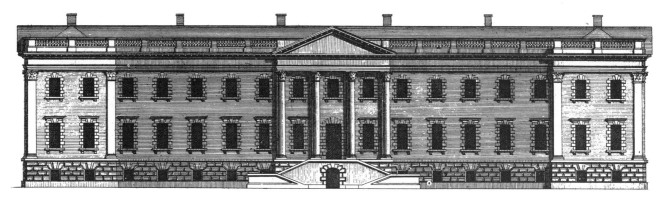

Principal Front

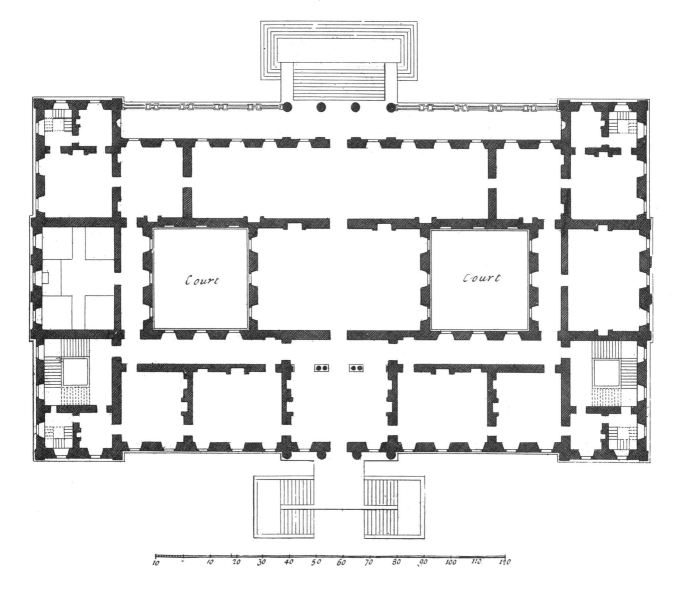

Court   Court

10   10   20   30   40   50   60   70   80   90   100   110   120

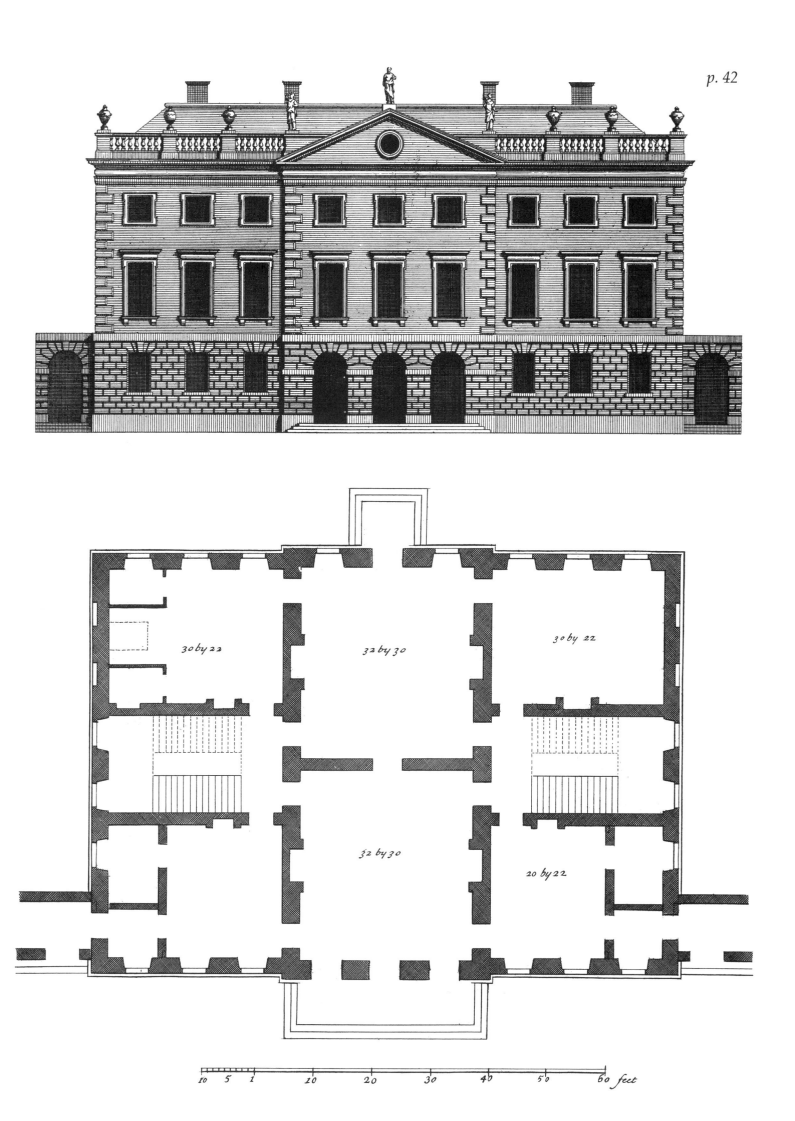

30 by 22   32 by 30   30 by 22

32 by 30   20 by 22

10 5 1   10   20   30   40   50   60 feet

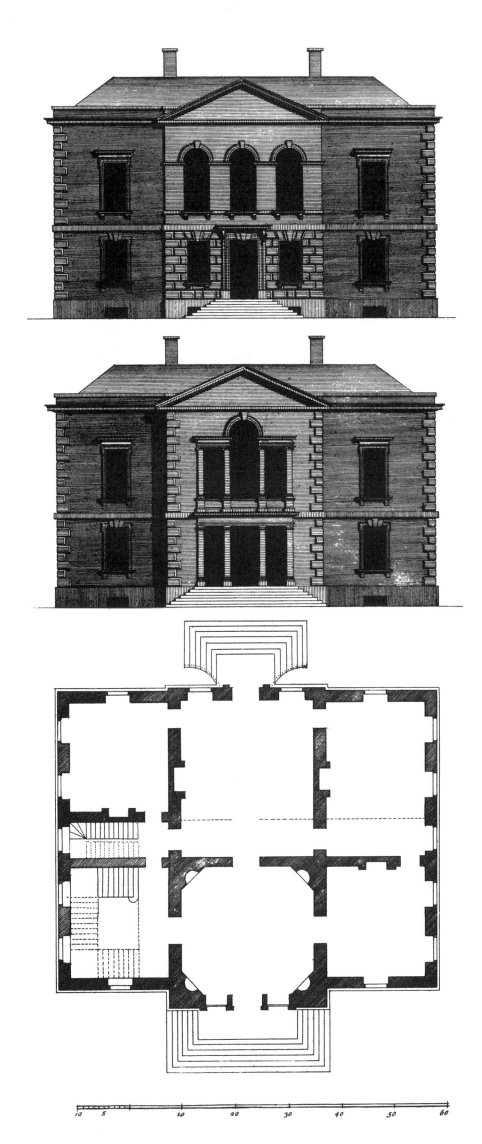

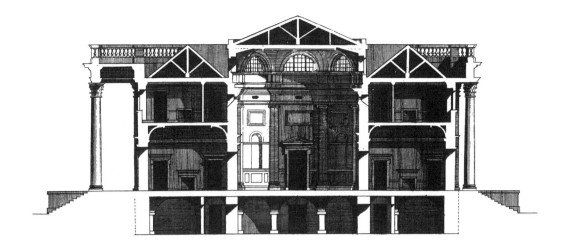

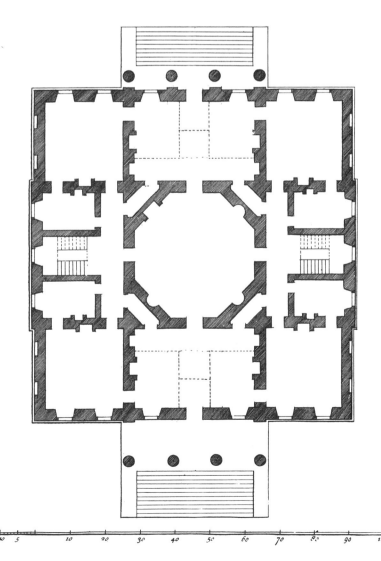

10 5   10   20   30   40   50   60   70   80   90   100

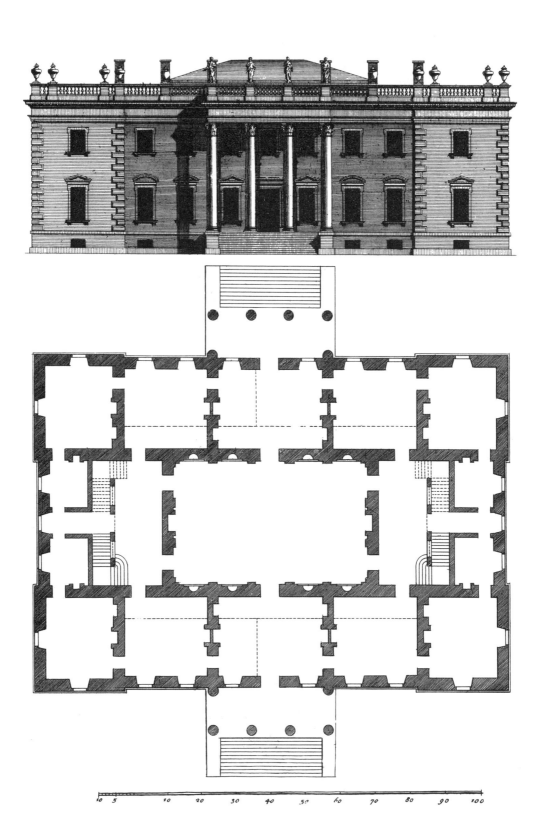

10 5   10   20   30   40   50   60   70   80   90   100

Court

Court

10 5 10 20 30 40 50 60 70 80 90 100 110 120 feet

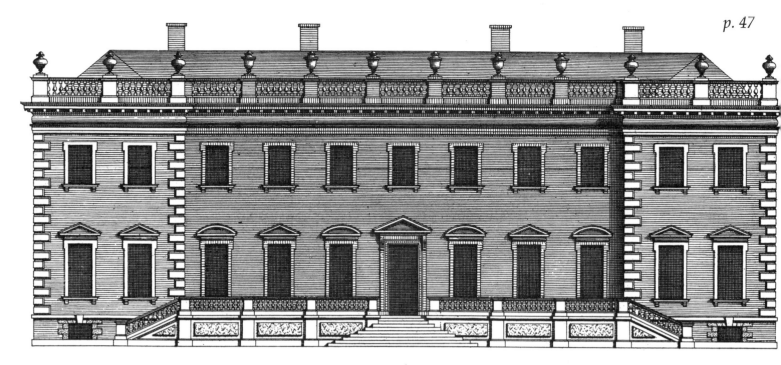

Fronting y.^e Garden.

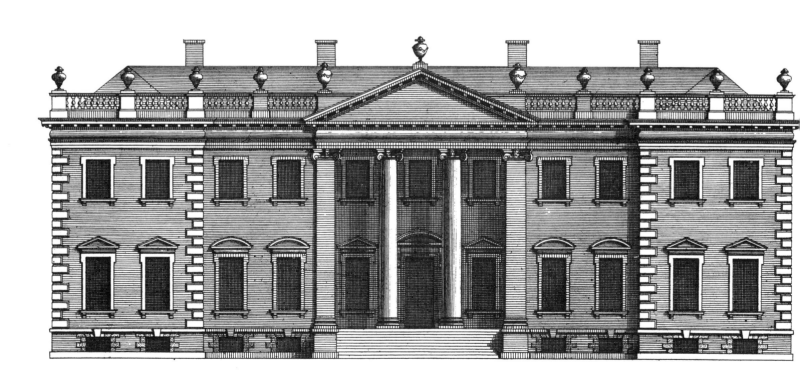

10 5   10   20   30   40   50   60   70   80

Fronting y.^e Court

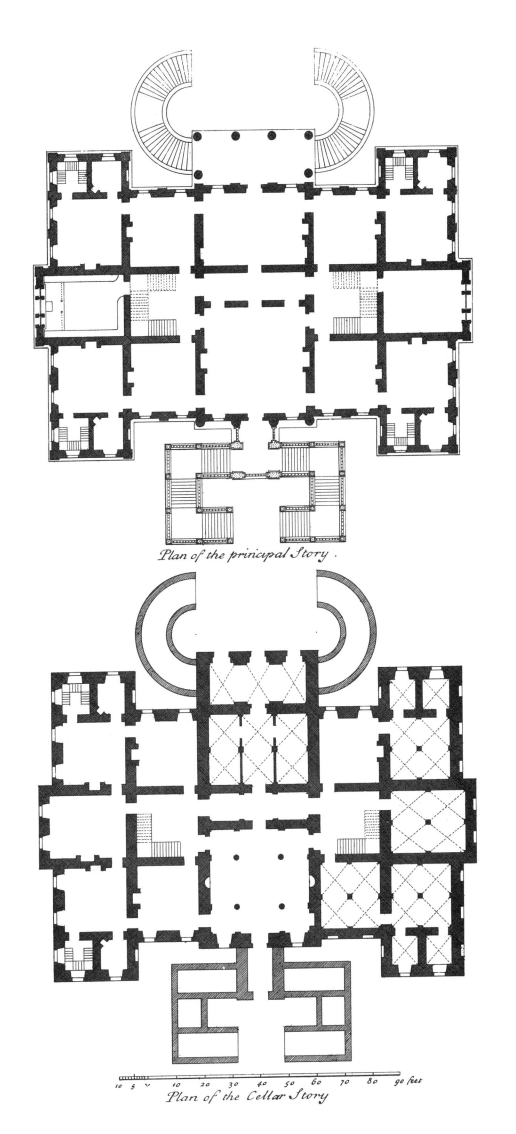

Plan of the principal Story.

Plan of the Cellar Story

Section.

Front towards the Garden.

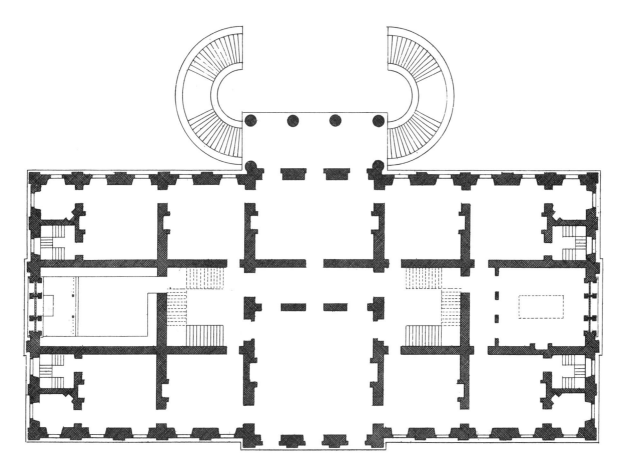

Plan of the principal Story.

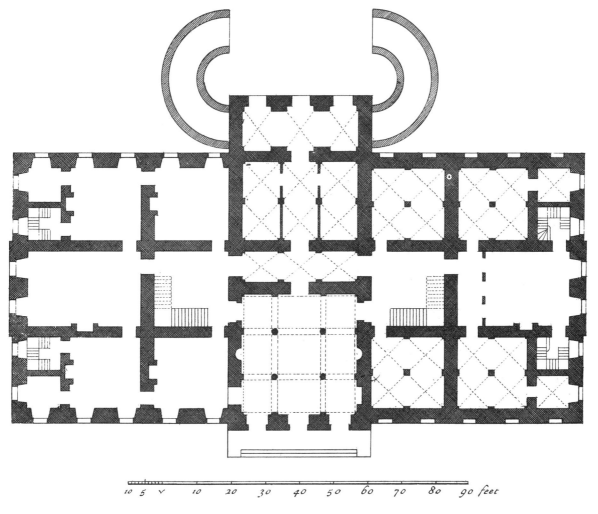

10 5 V 10 20 30 40 50 60 70 80 90 feet

The Cellar Story.

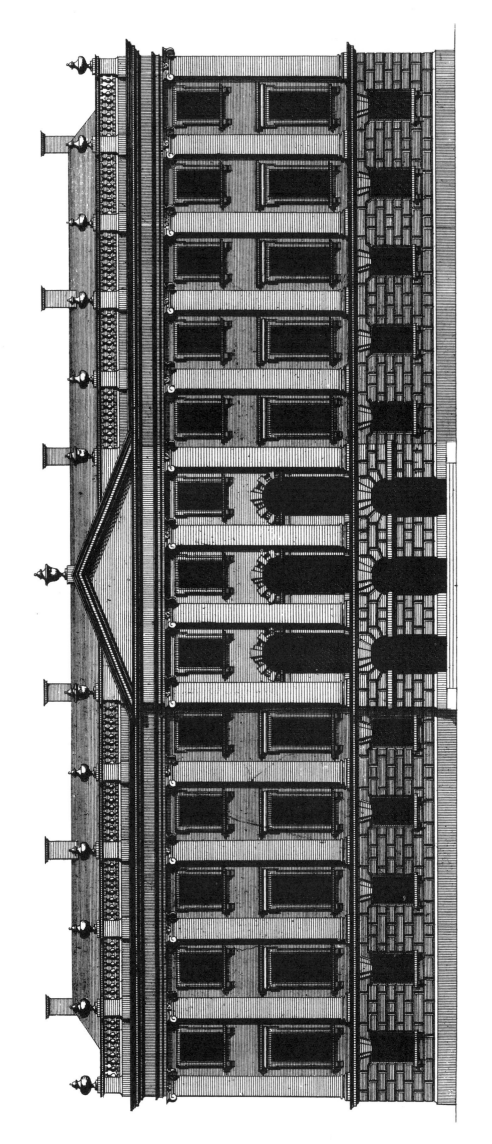

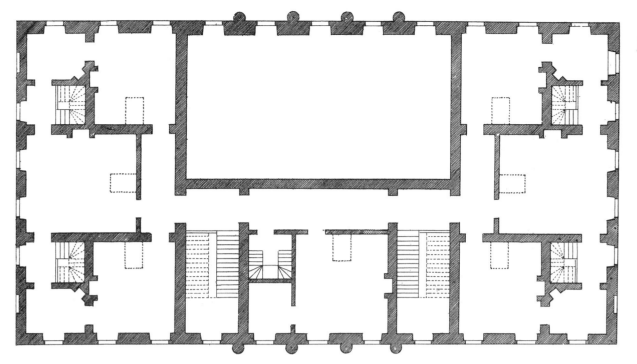

The one pair of Stairs

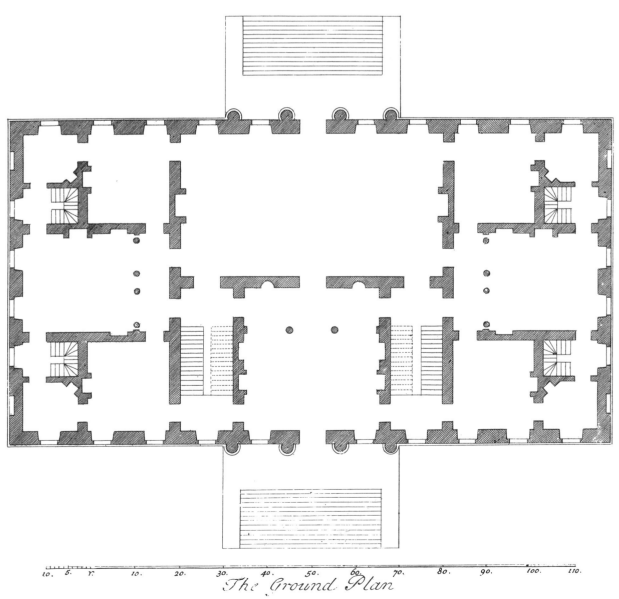

The Ground Plan

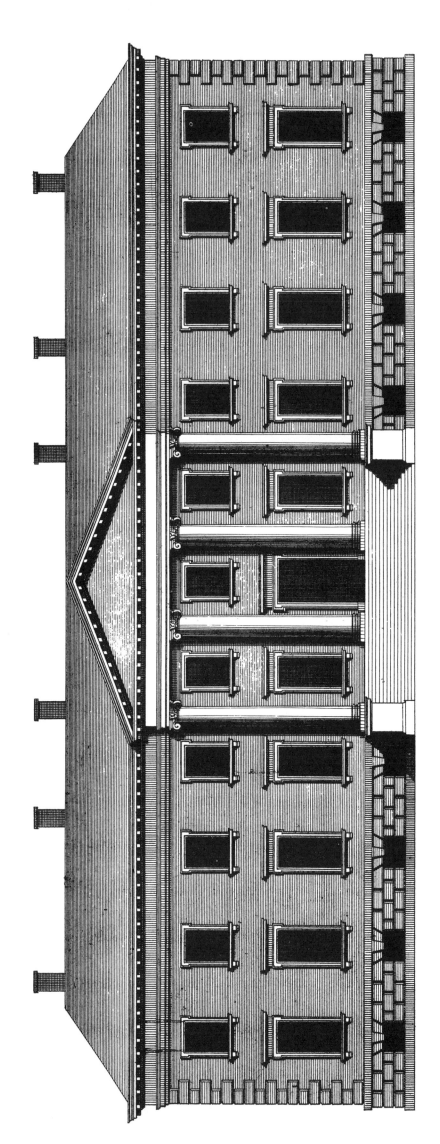

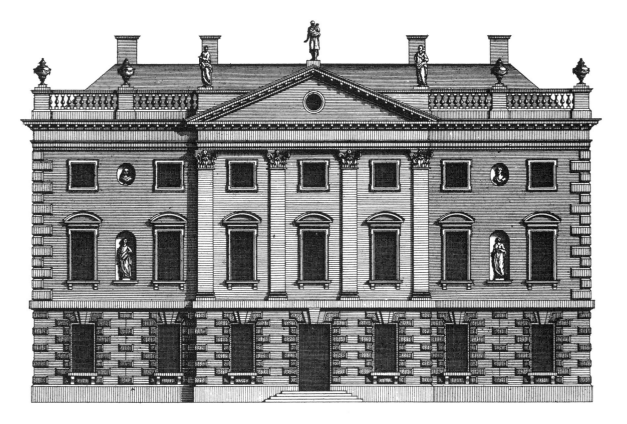

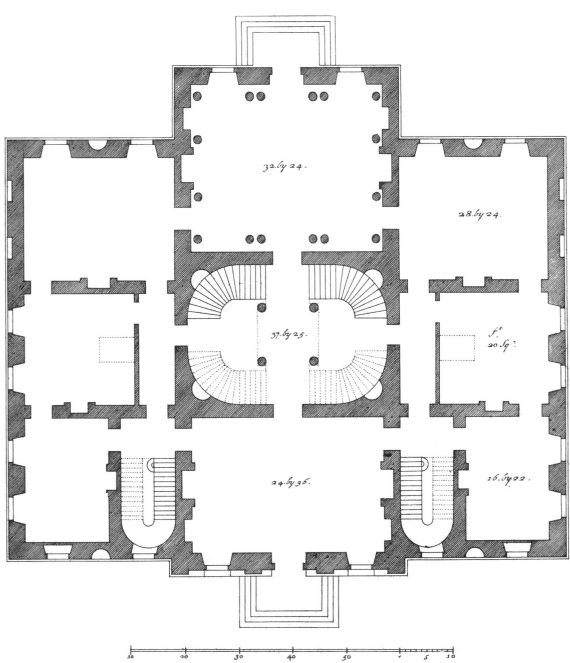

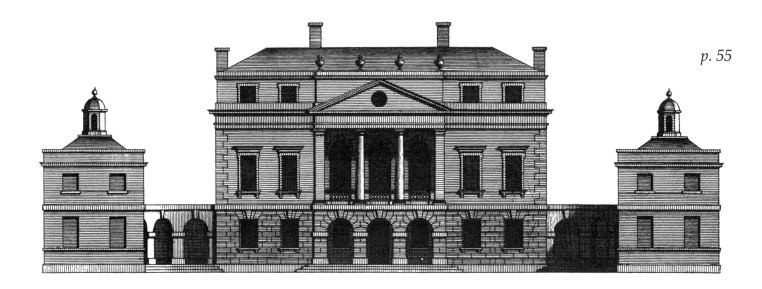

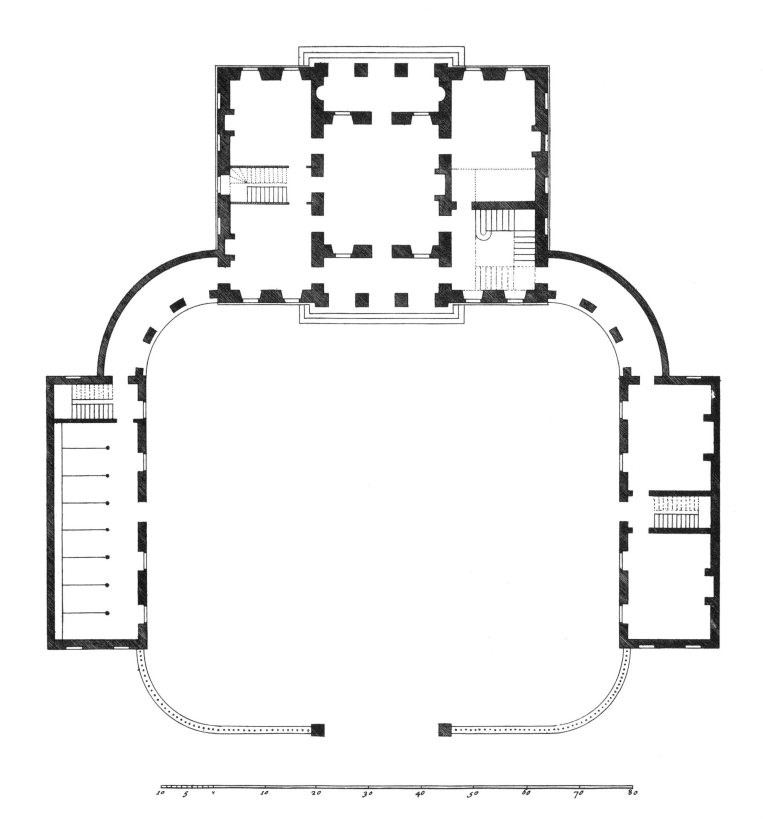

10 5 v 10 20 30 40 50 60 70 80

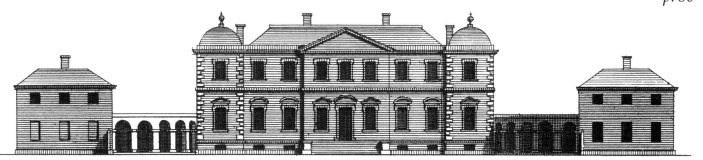

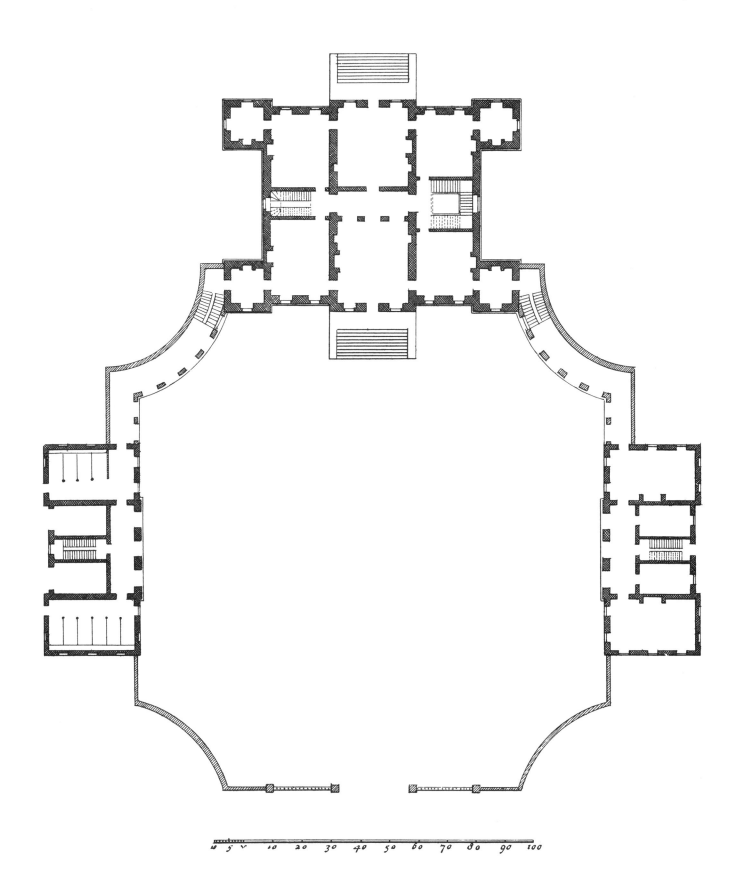

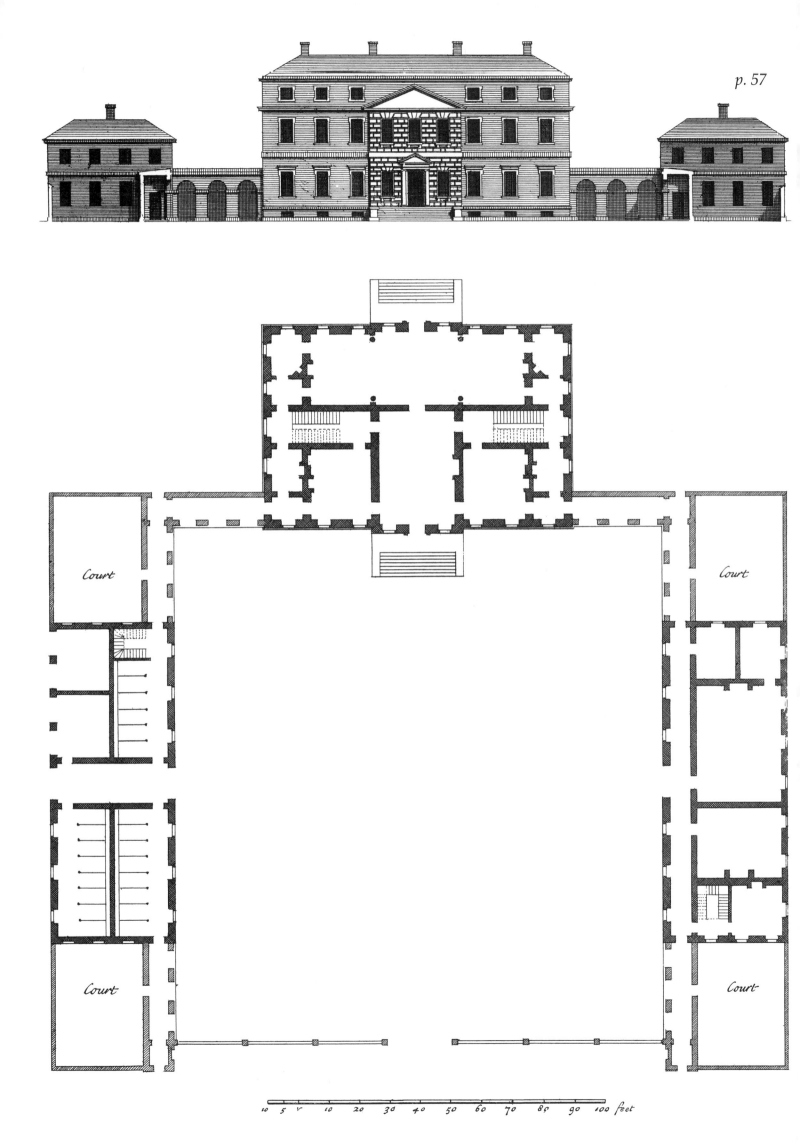

Court

Court

Court

Court

10 5 0   10   20   30   40   50   60   70   80   90   100 feet

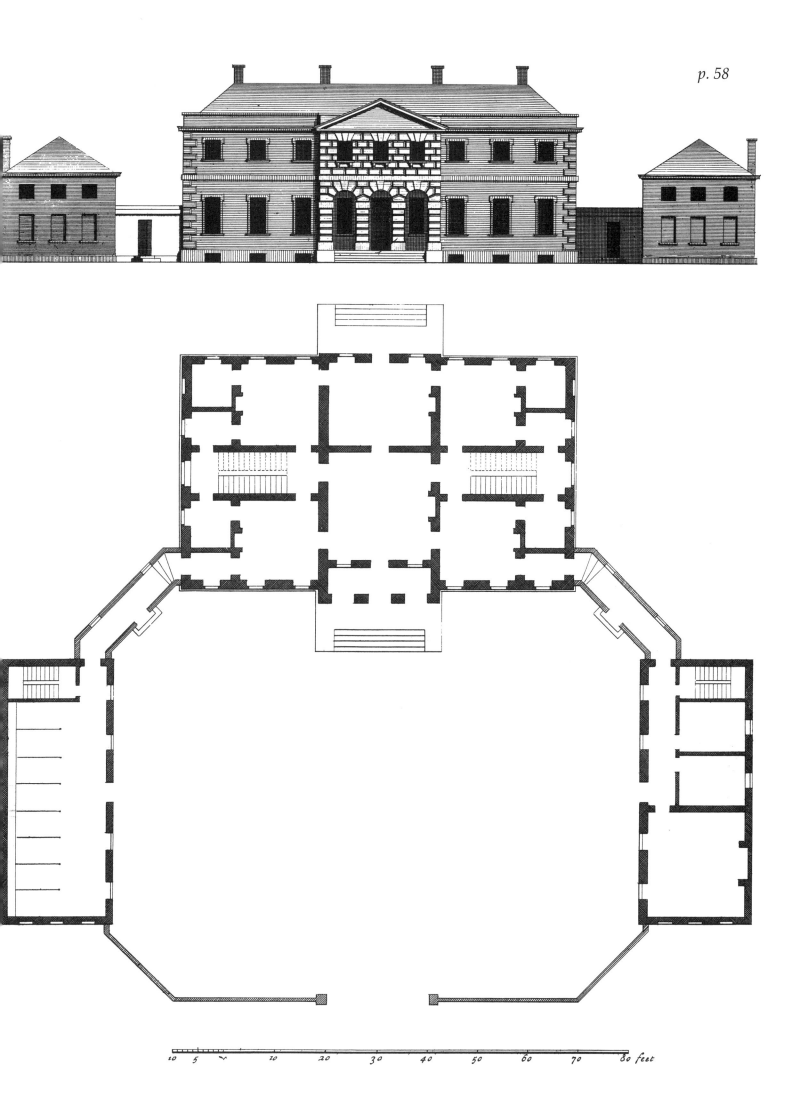

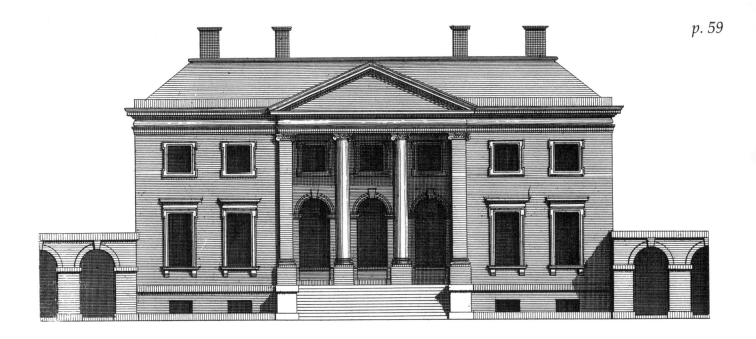

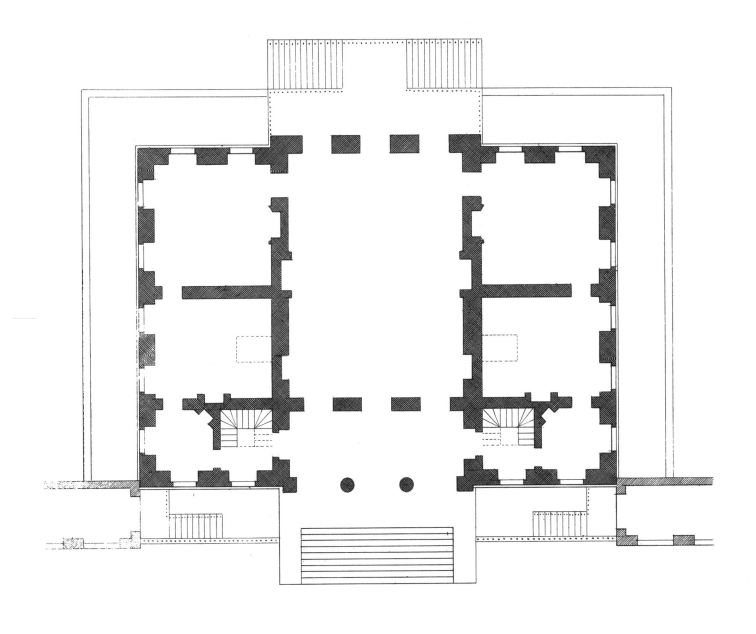

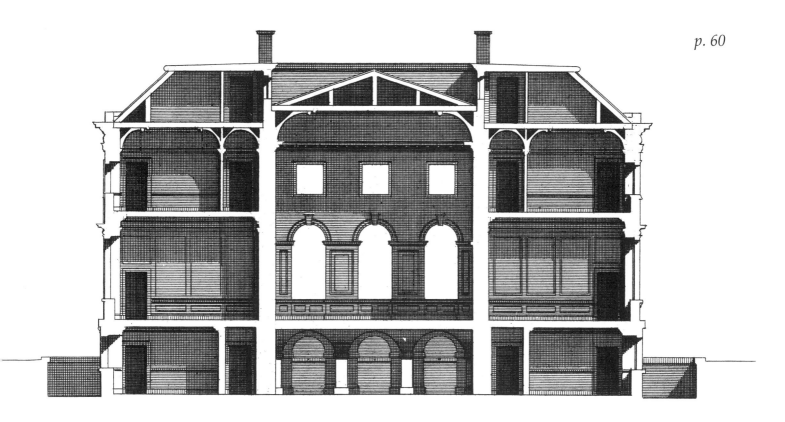

Section of the fore going house.

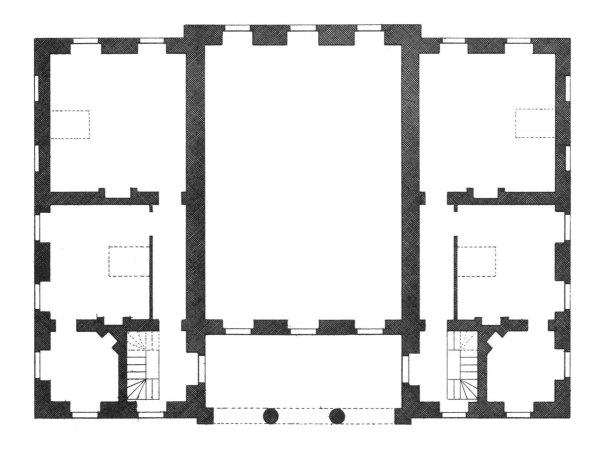

The Plan of the Second floore.

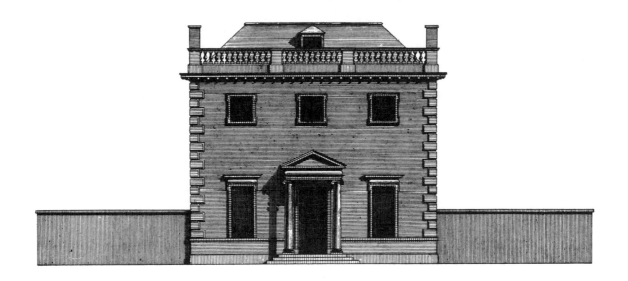

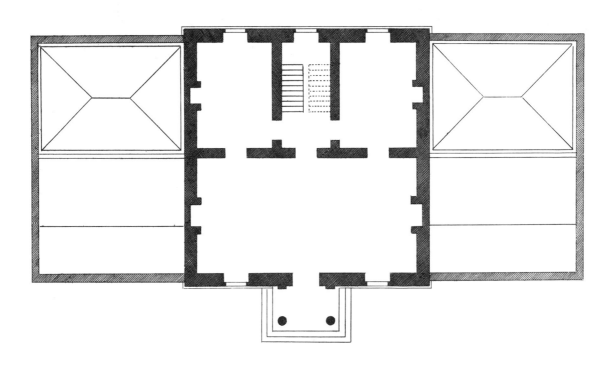

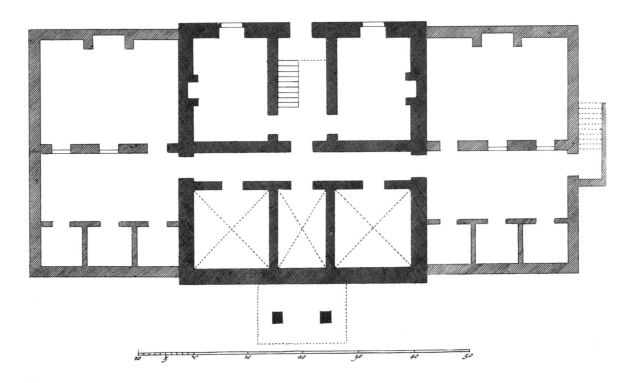

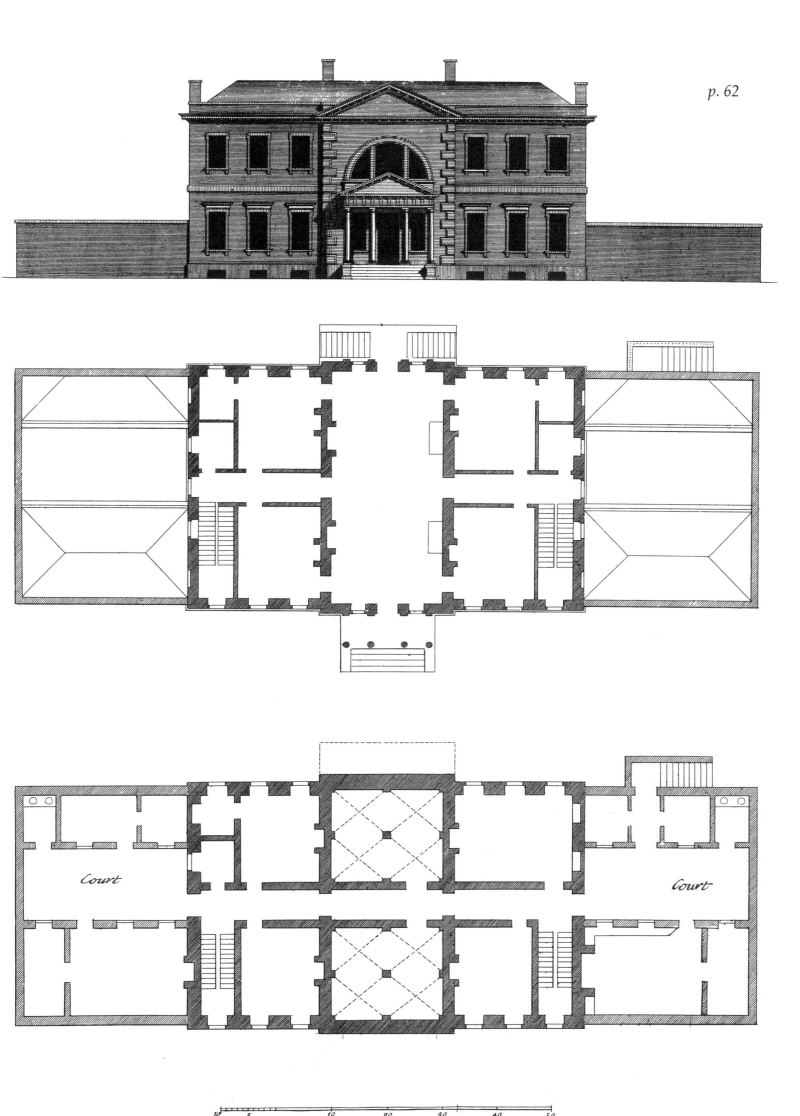

Court

Court

10 5 10 20 30 40 50

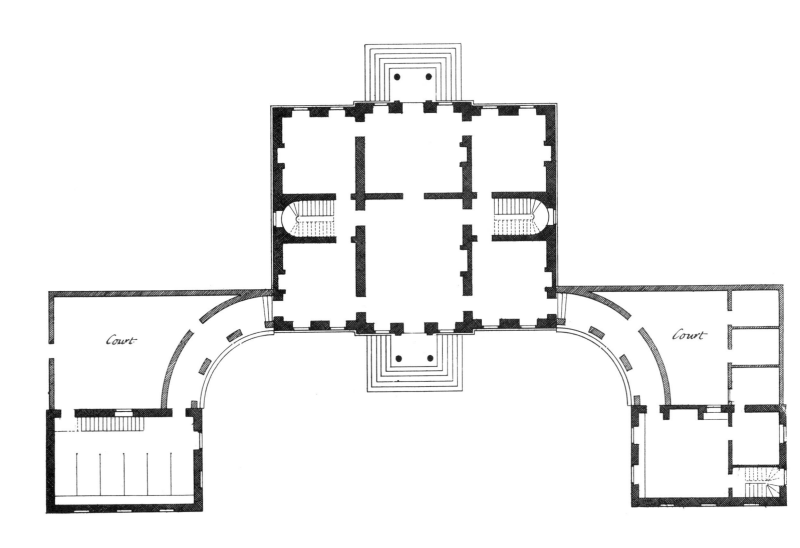

Court

Court

10 5 v 10 20 30 40 50 60 70 80 feet

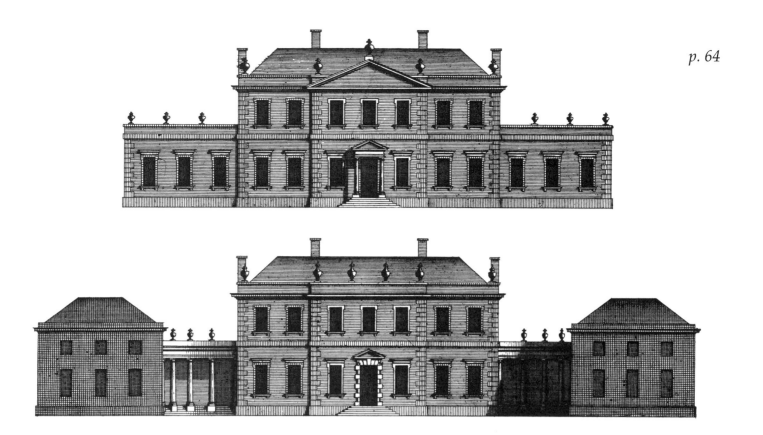

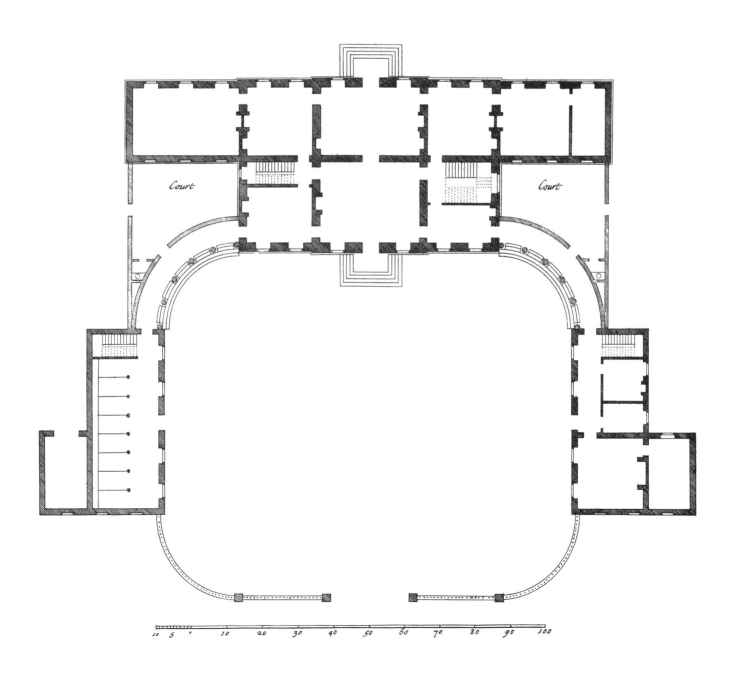

Court   Court

10 5   10   20   30   40   50   60   70   80   90   100

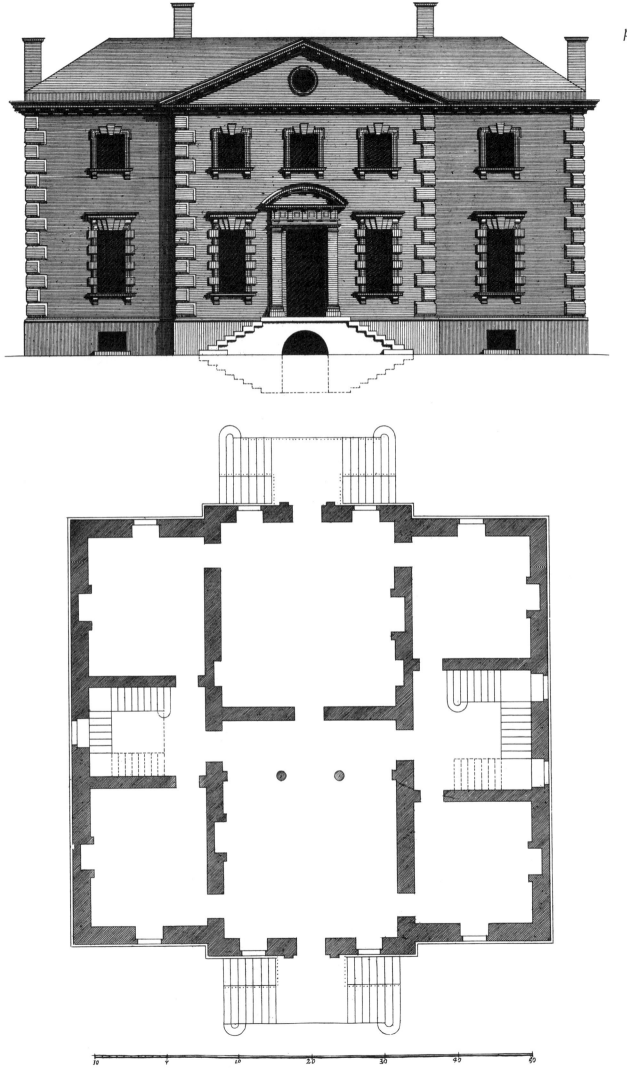

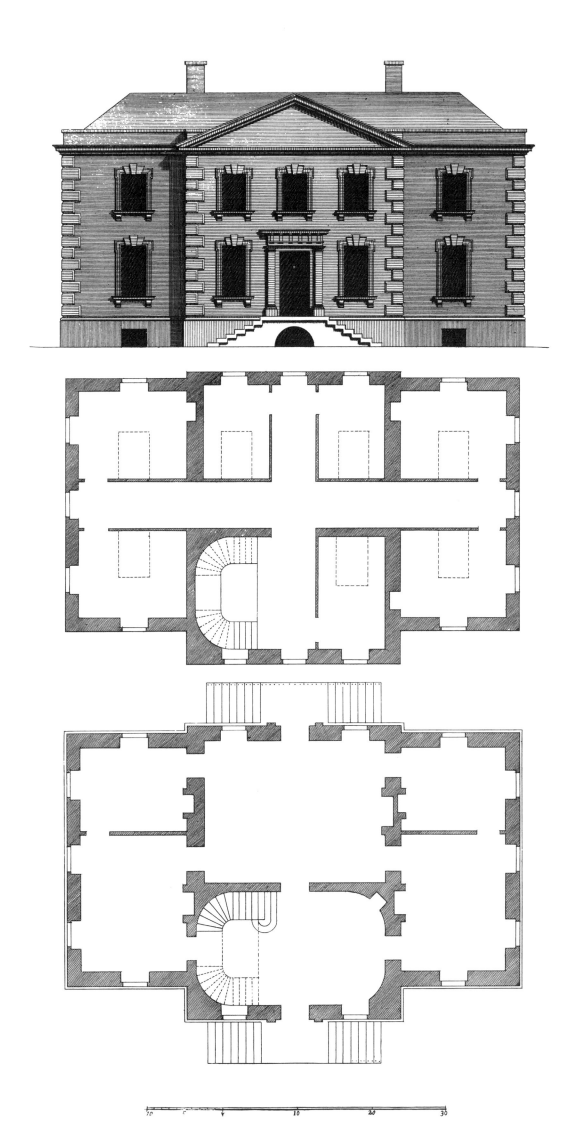

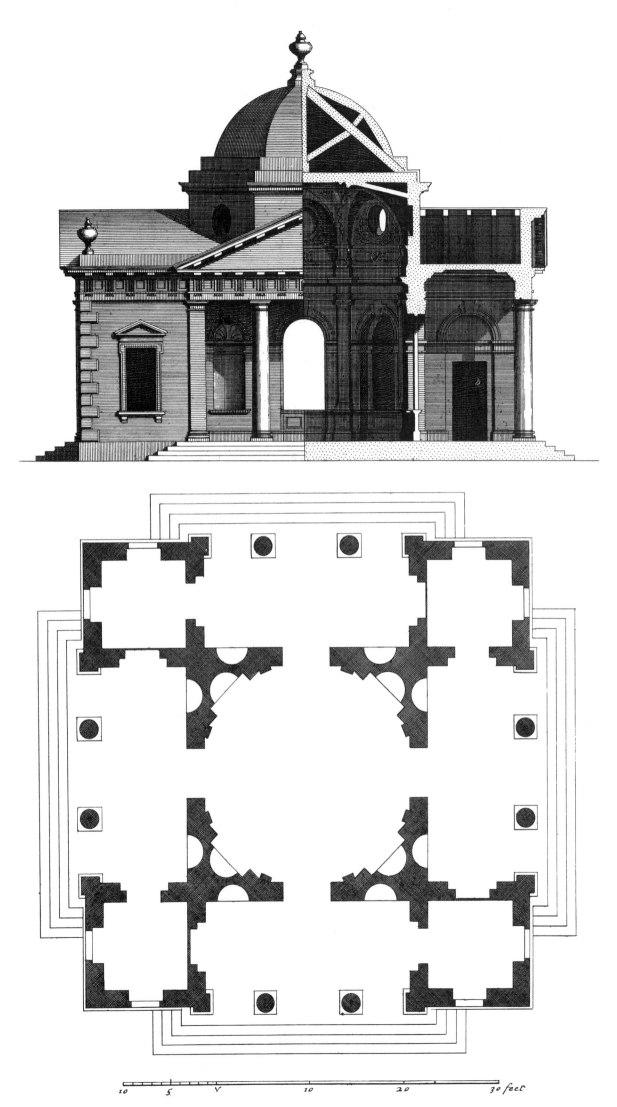

10   5   V   10   20   30 feet

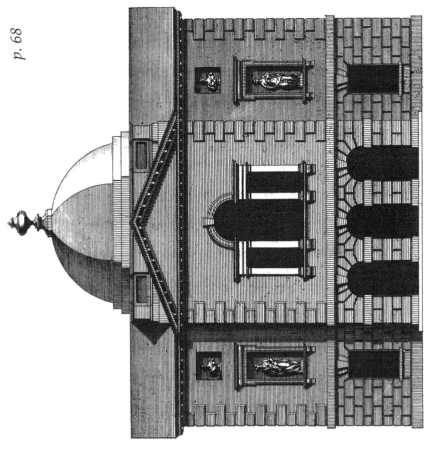
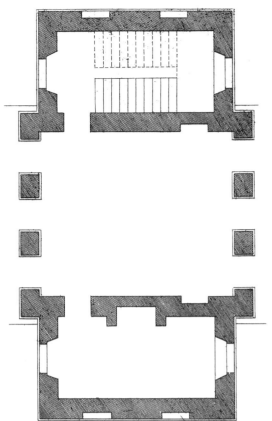
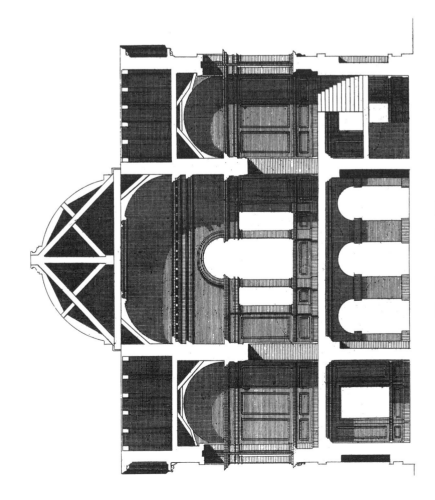
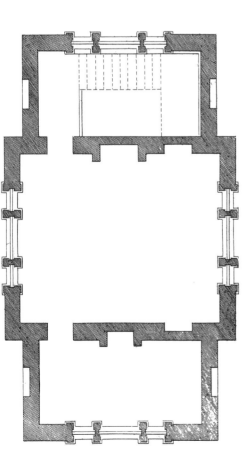

30 feet

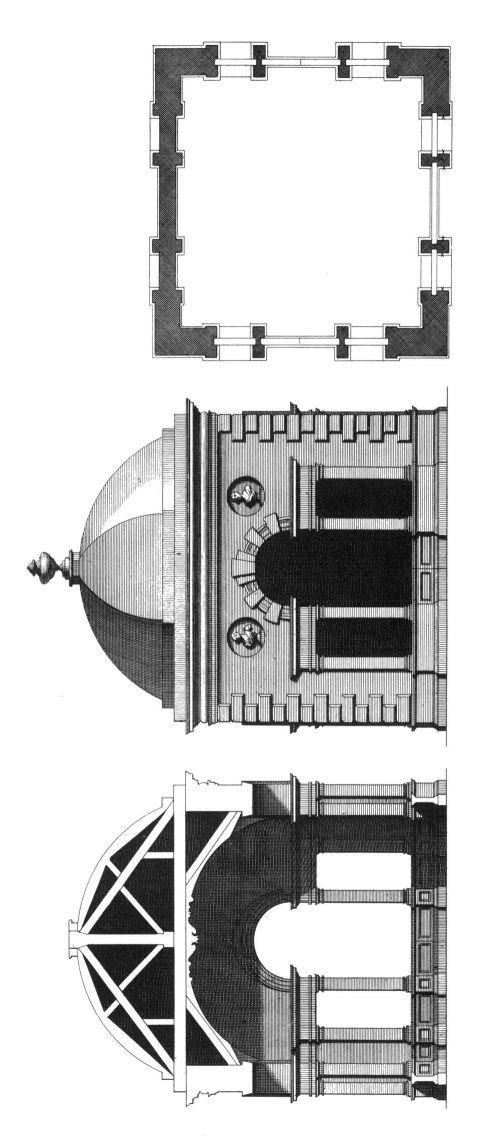

30 feet

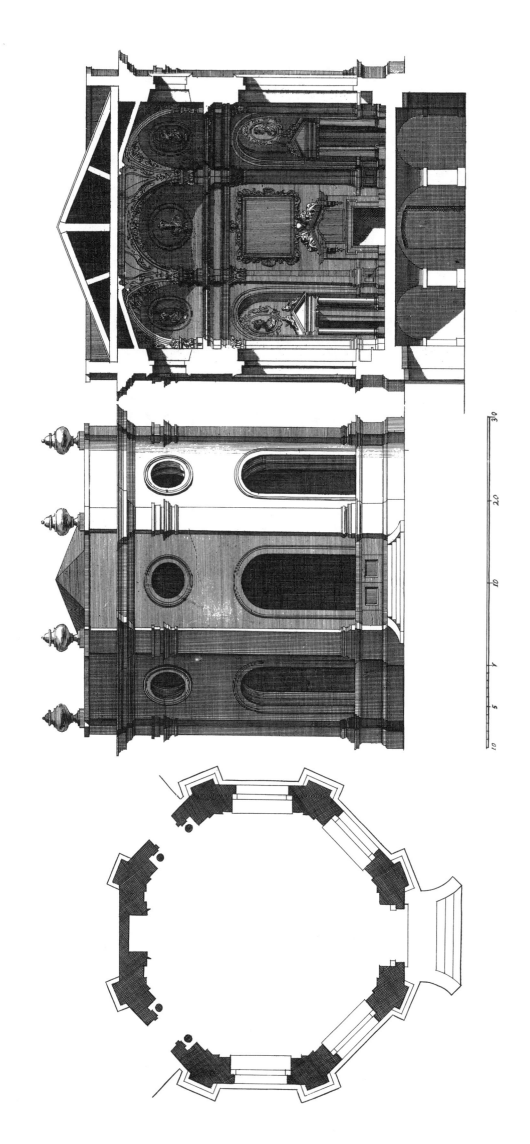

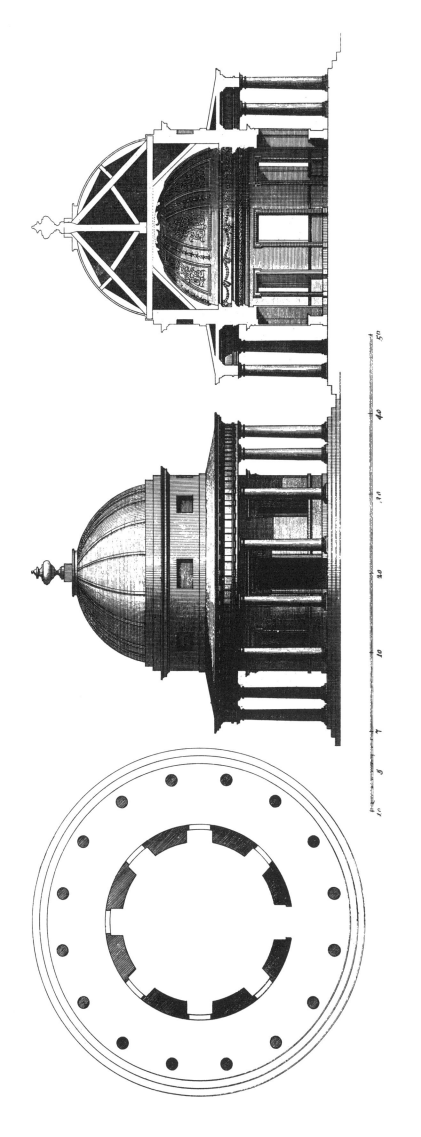

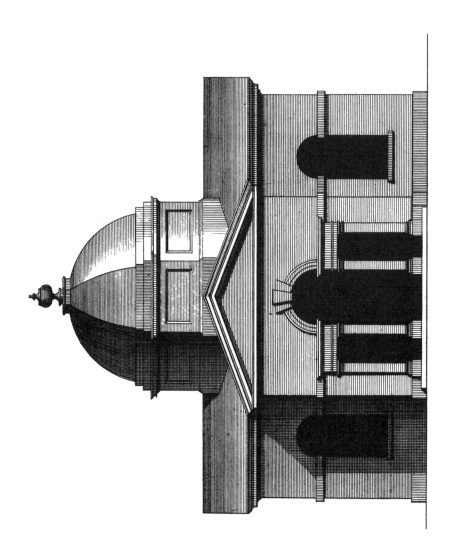

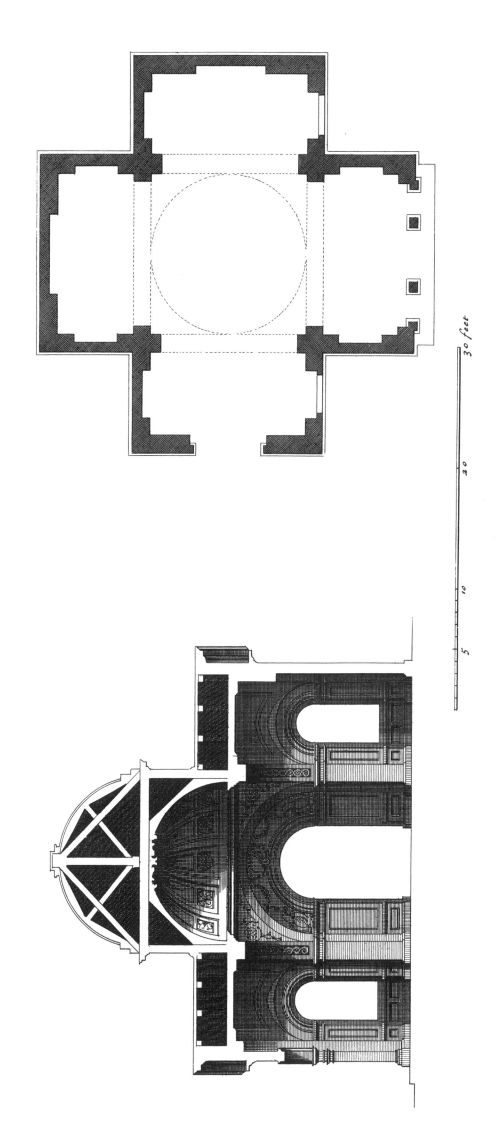

30 feet

20

10

5

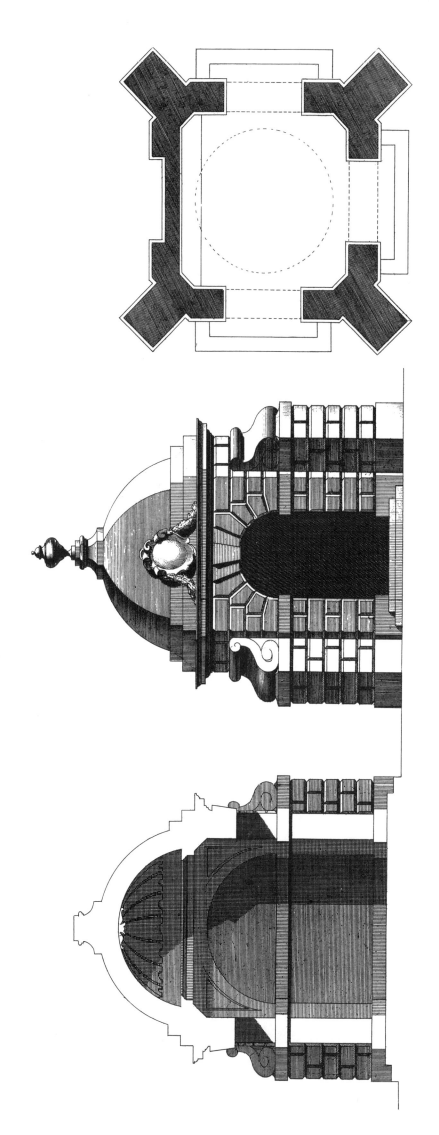

10 5   10   20   30 feet

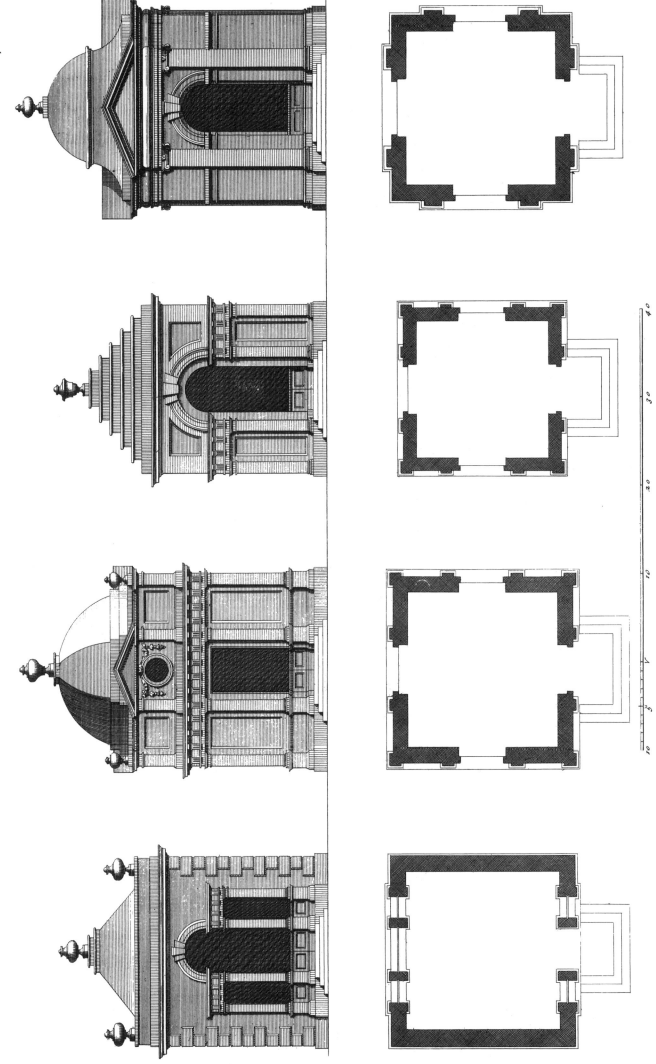

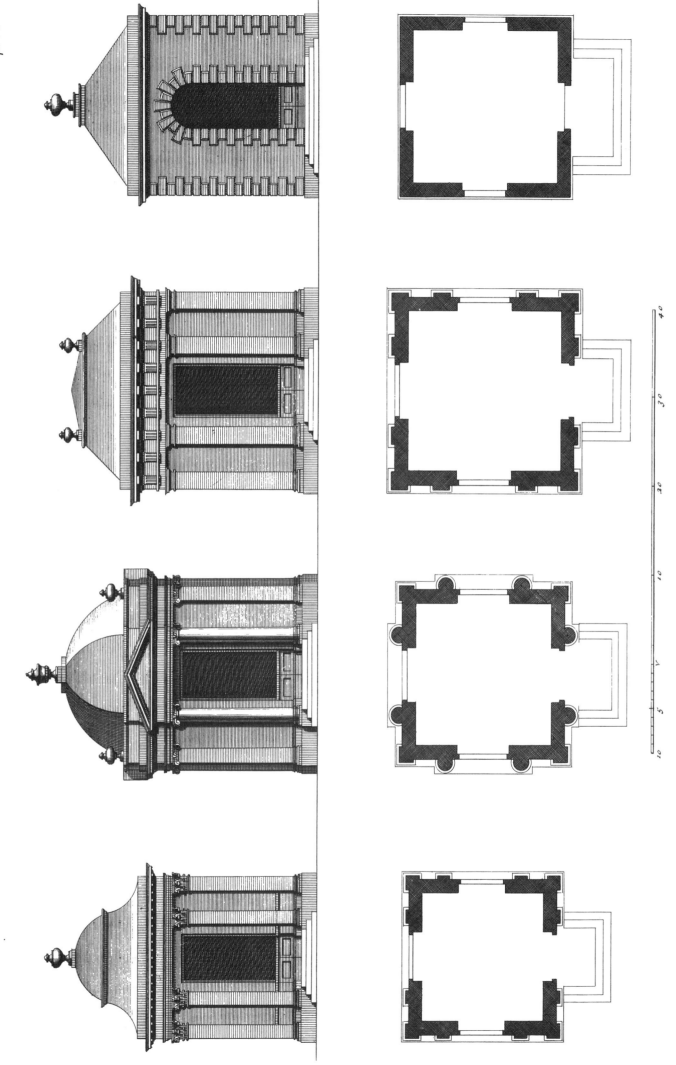

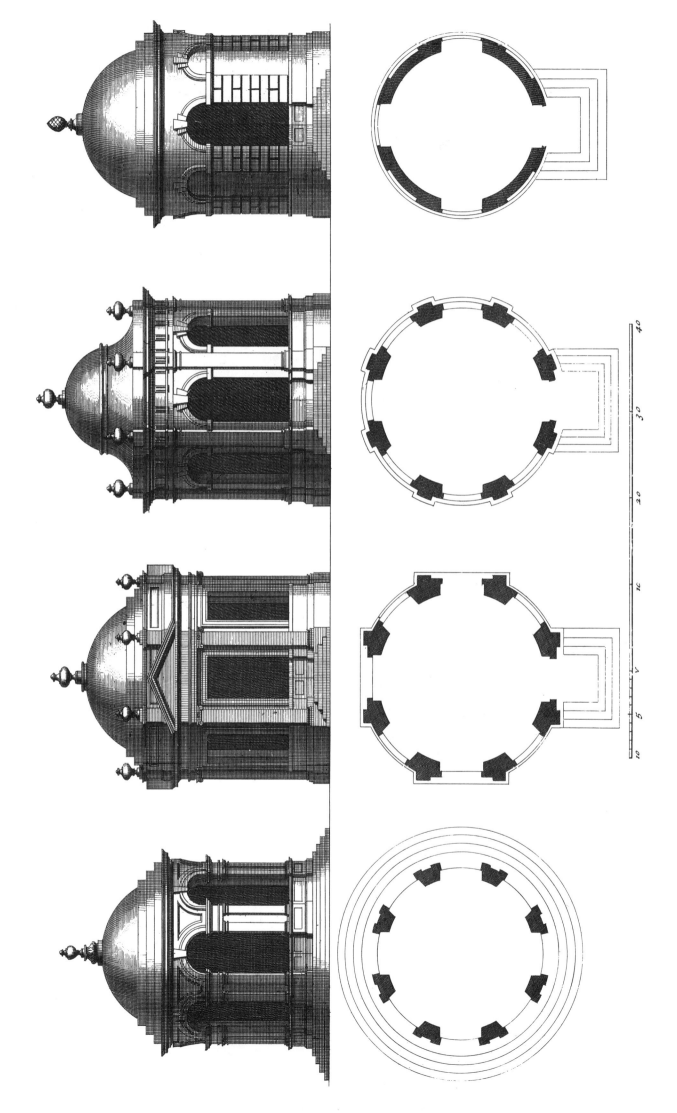

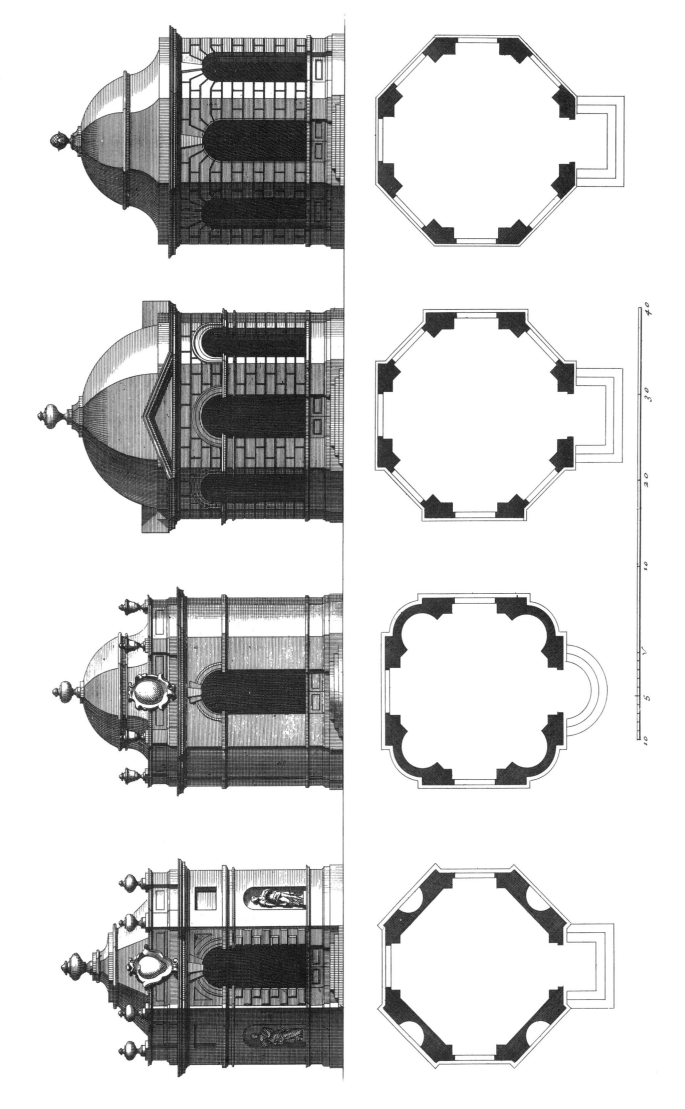

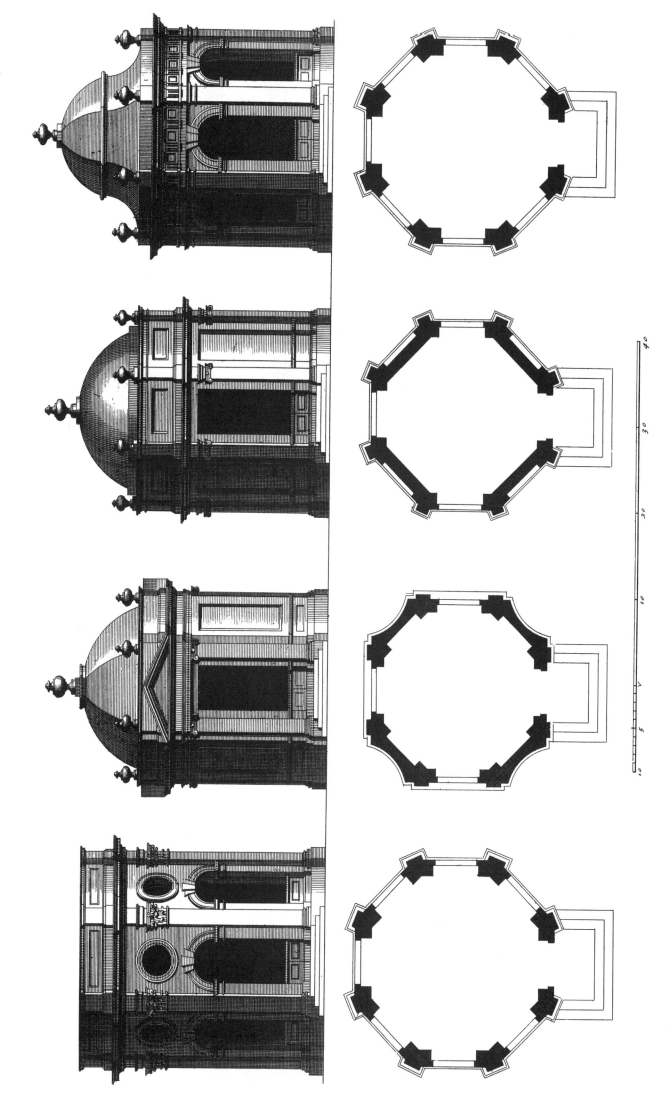

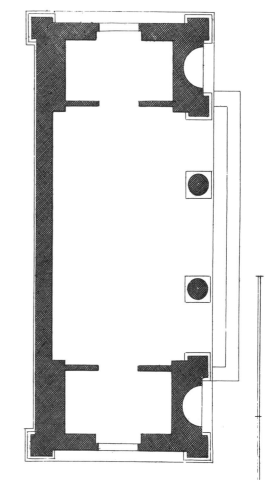
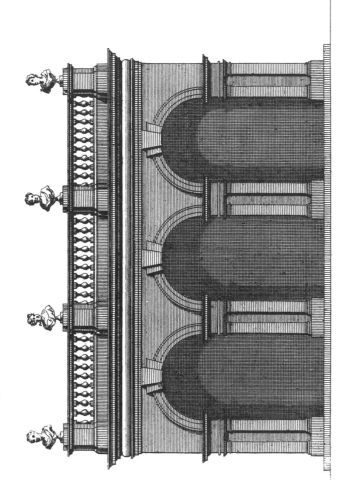
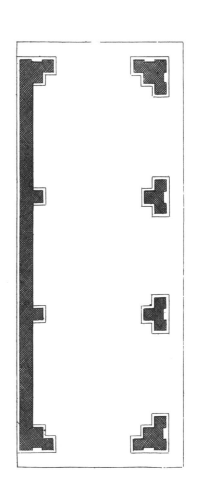

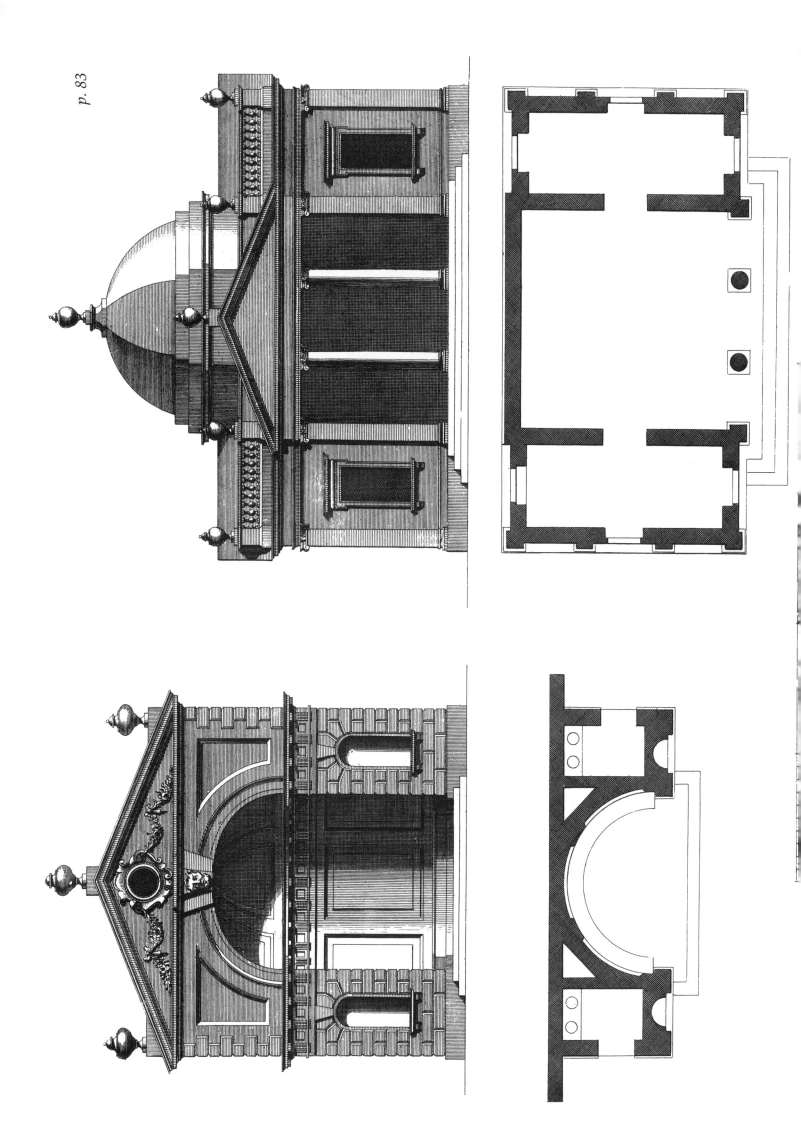

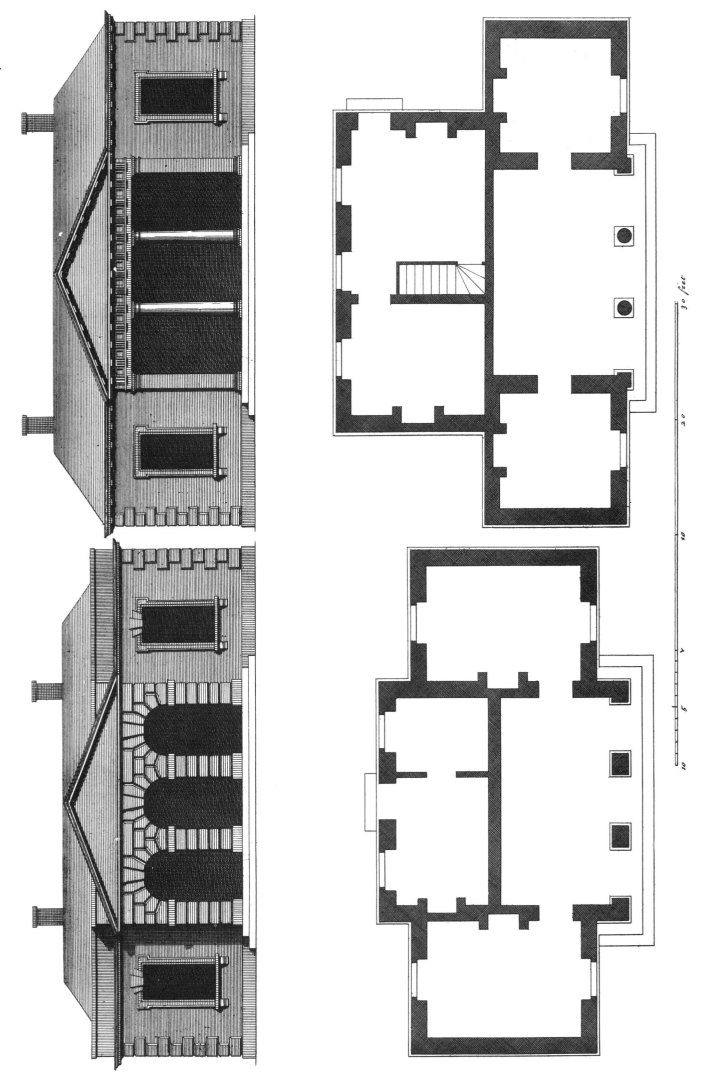

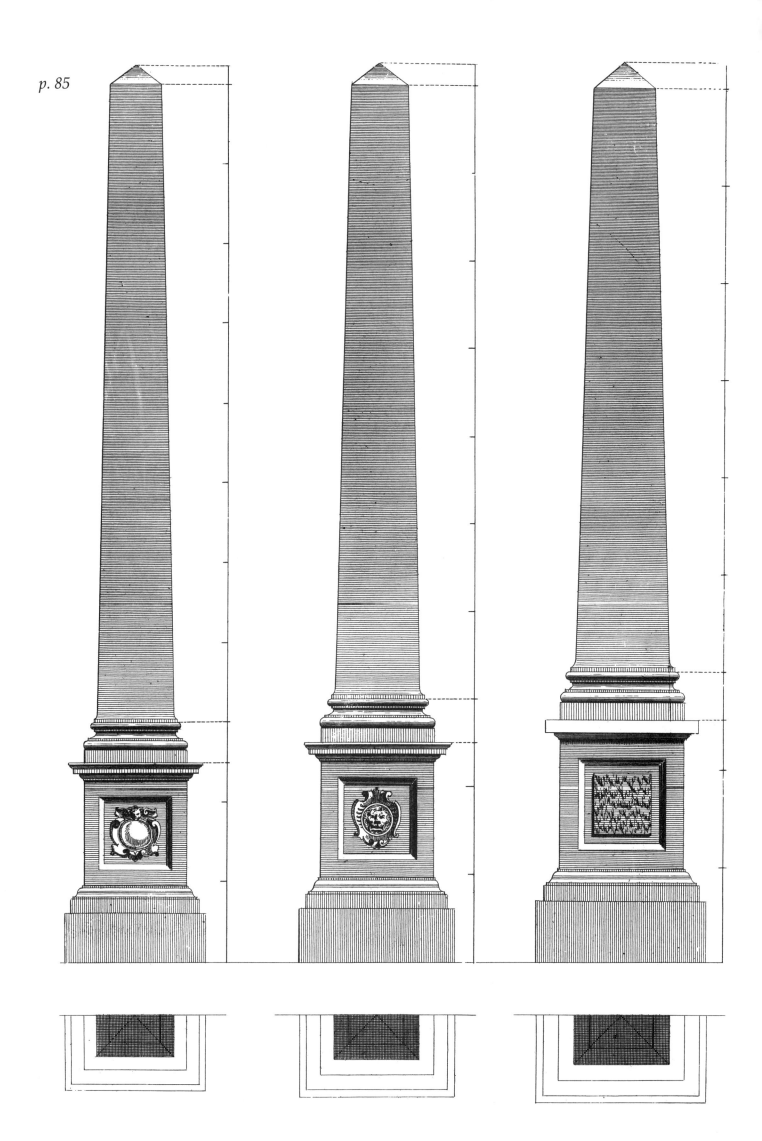

p. 86

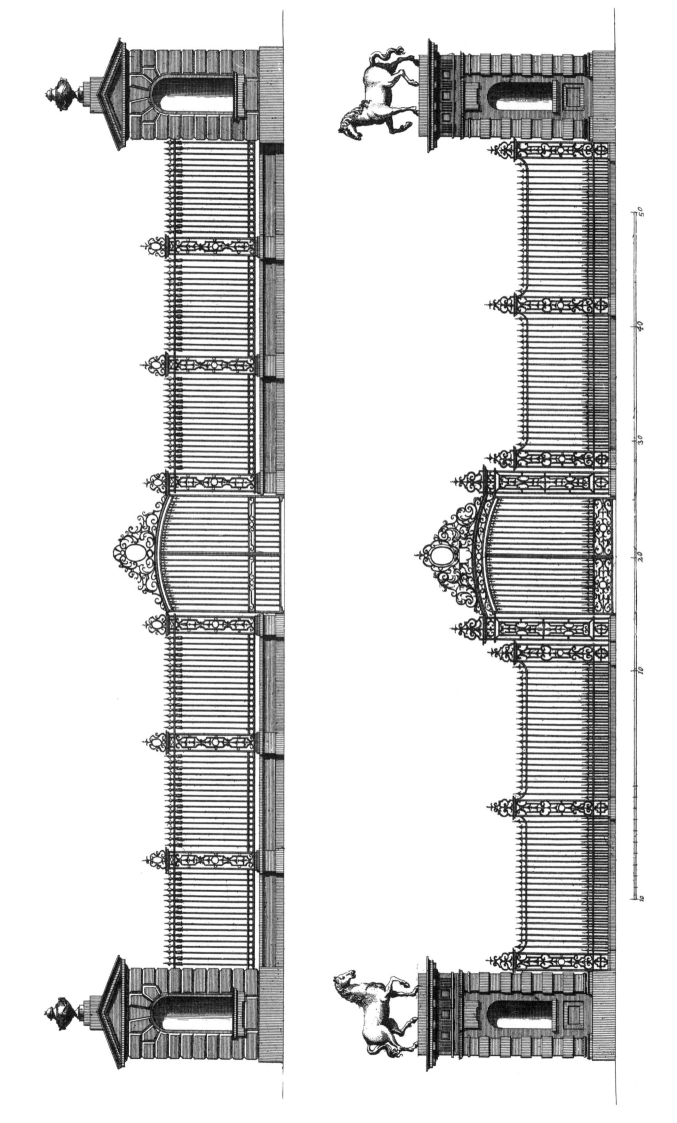

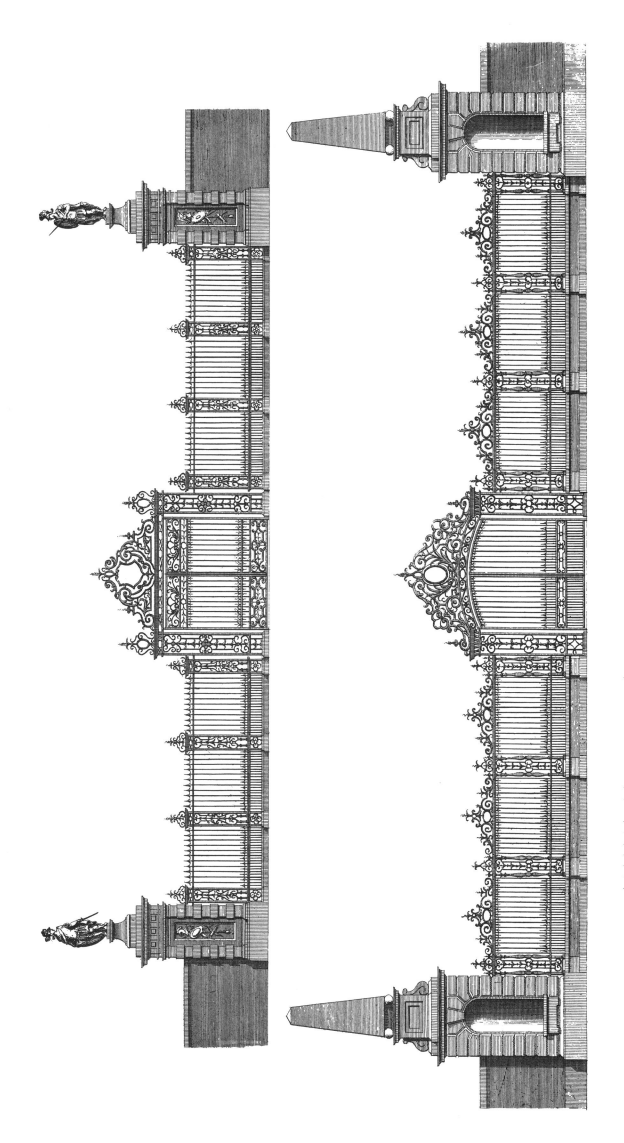

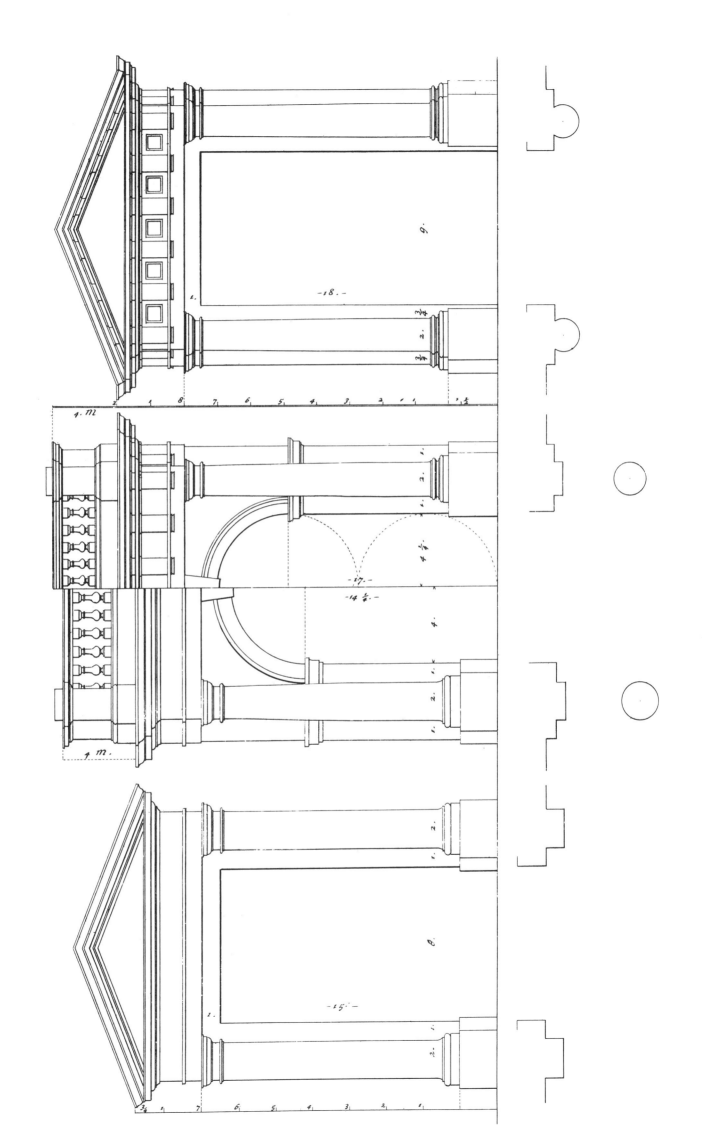

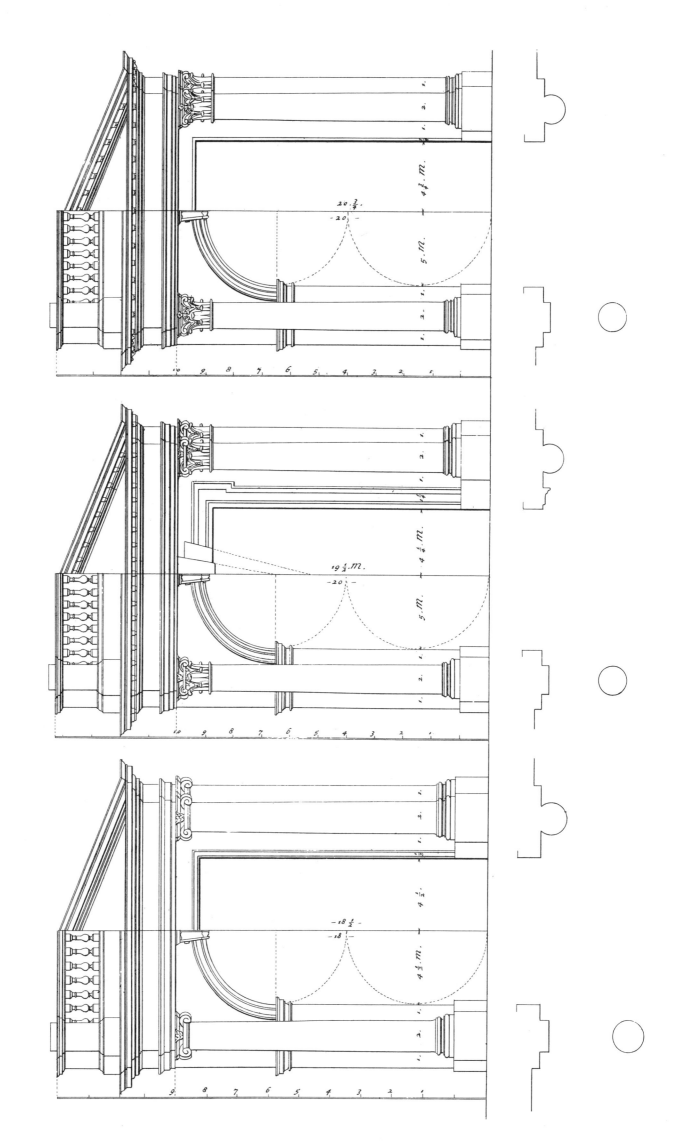

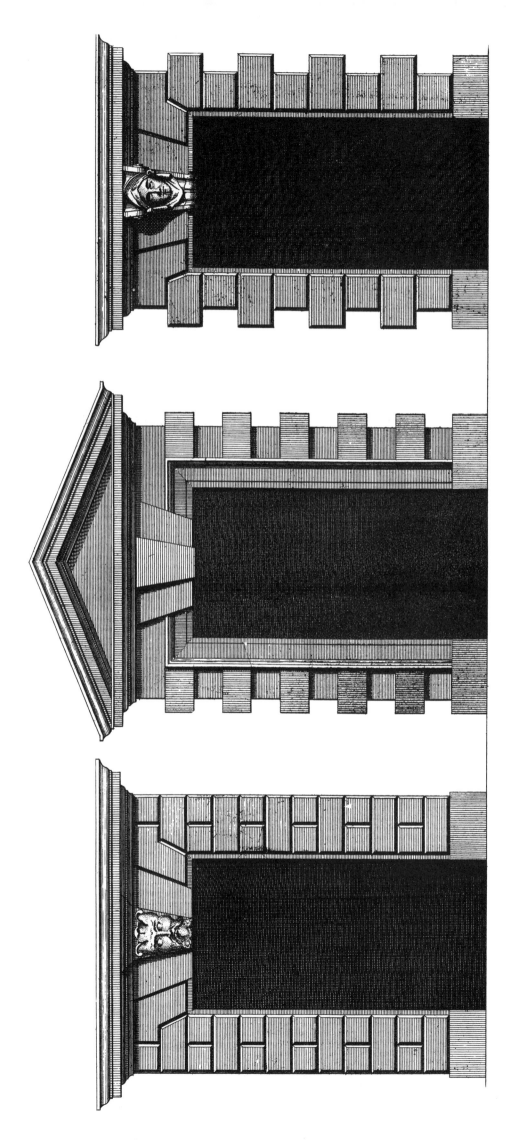

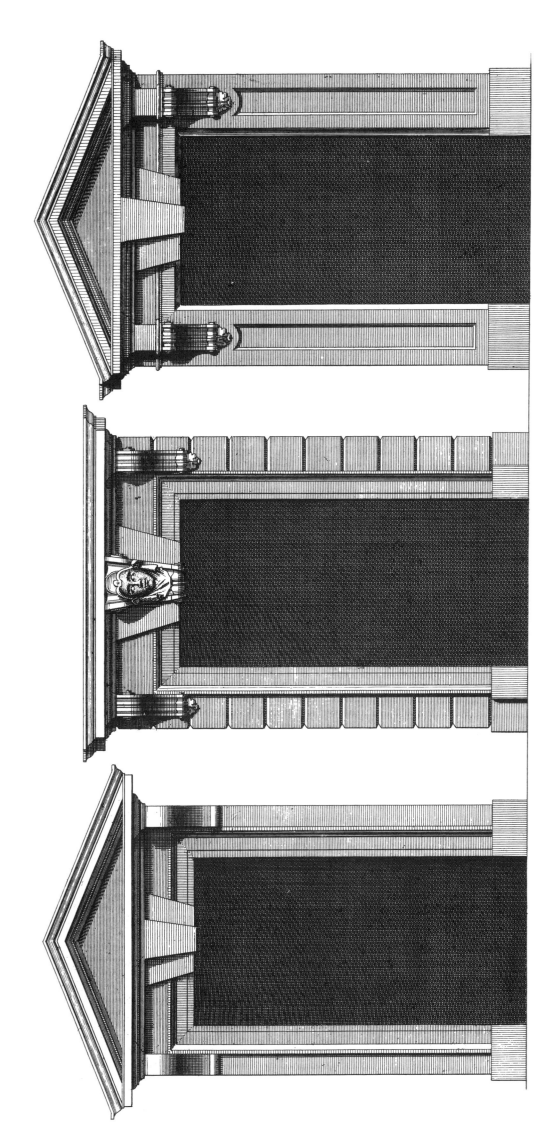

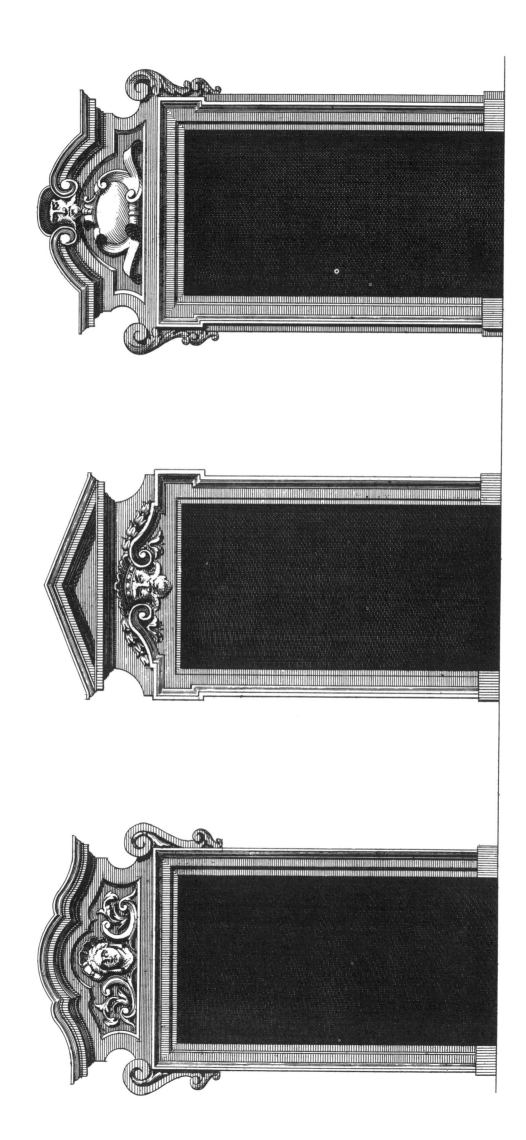

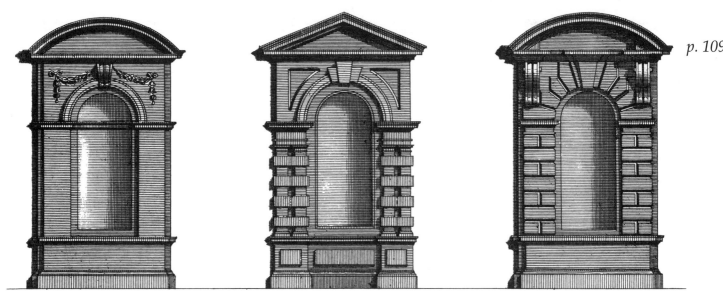

To the Right Hon.ble the Lady HENRIETTA CAVENDISHE HOLLES
Countefs of OXFORD *&* Countefs MORTIMER.

*This Design being made & executed by your Ladyfhips special Direction is now humbly
presented by your Ladyfhips most Dutyfull & Obedient Servant*

Wilk.

To the R.t Hon.ble Edward Earl of Oxford & Earl Mortimer,
This Plate is humbly Dedicated by his Lordships most Obedient Ser.t Ja: Gibbs.

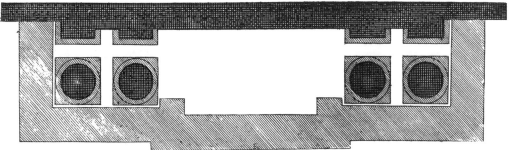

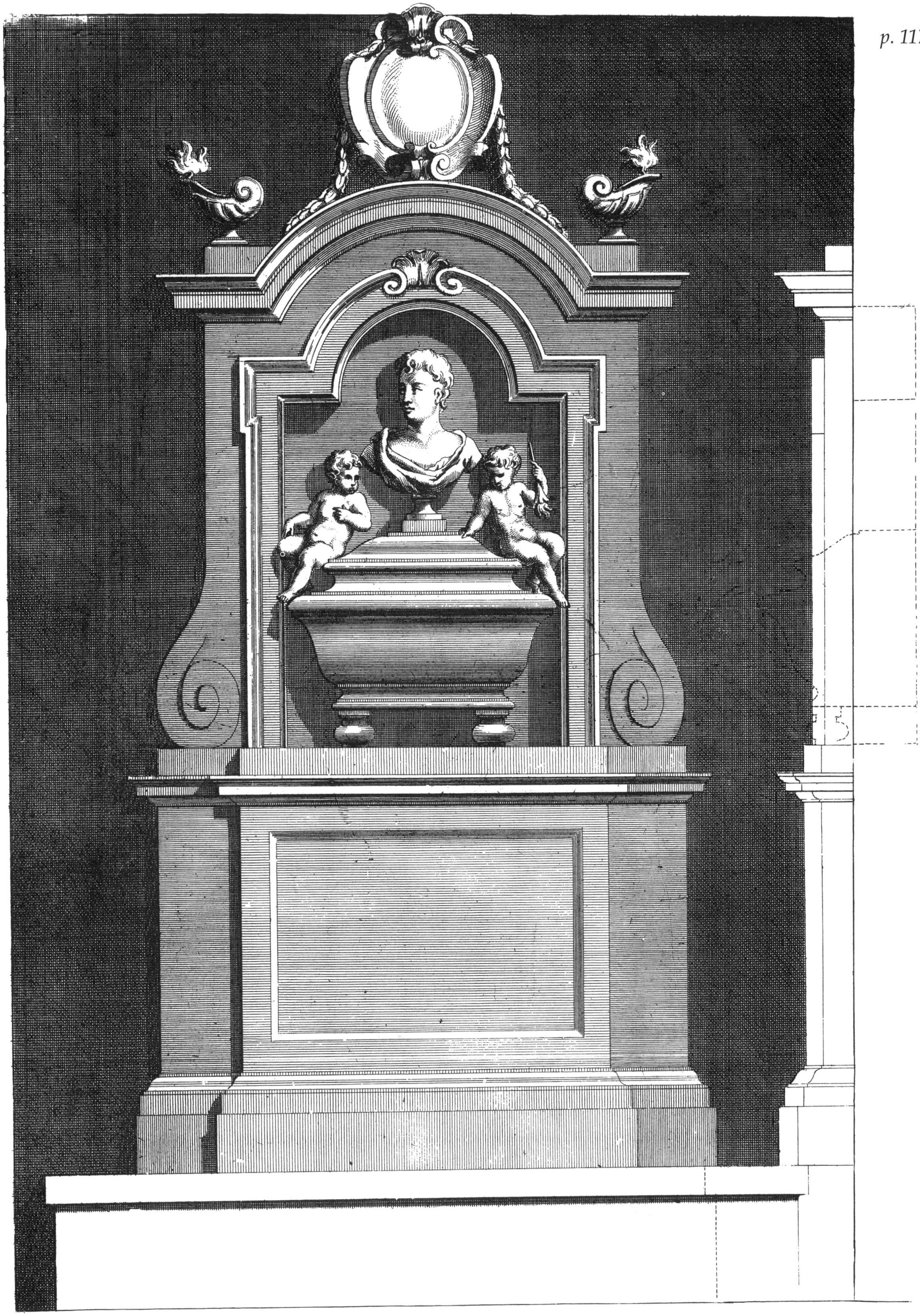

Æternæ Memoriæ Sacrum.

Lectissimæ Matronæ D. SOPHIÆ FAIRHOLM ANNANDIÆ
Marchionissæ, SCOTIA ortæ; Cujus ingenii morumqᵗ
elegantia cum eximia corporis forma certabat; Matris Uxorisqᵗ
laudibus inclytæ; tam diligentis autem Matris familias, ut
oblatam rerum domesticarum molem animo virili et negotiis
pari sustinuerit; Tot denique virtutibus ornatæ ut vitam summâ
omnium cum admiratione morte omnibus deplorata finiverit;
Monumentum hoc, qualecumqᵗ pietatis gratiqᵗ animi
indicium, mœrens posuit IAC: IO: fil: na. max. ANNANDLÆ
Marchio: Obiit 13. Dec. Anno Dñi. 1716.
Ætatis 49.

Hic etiam jussu ejusdem MARCHIONIS reconditæ sunt
reliquiæ D. GULIELMI IOHNSTONE fratris sui charissimi
et filii natu secundi dictæ Marchionissæ, Qui obiit 24.
Dec: 1721. Anno Ætatis 26.

Ia: Gibbs Arch:

This Monument was erected in the South Isle of Westminster Abbey by the
Most Honᵇˡᵉ IAMES Lᵈ Marquis of ANNANDALE, to the Memory of
SOPHIA Marchioness of ANNANDALE his Mother, and
Lᵈ WILLIAM IOHNSTONE his younger Brother, Anno Dñi.
1723.

G. Vertue Sculp.

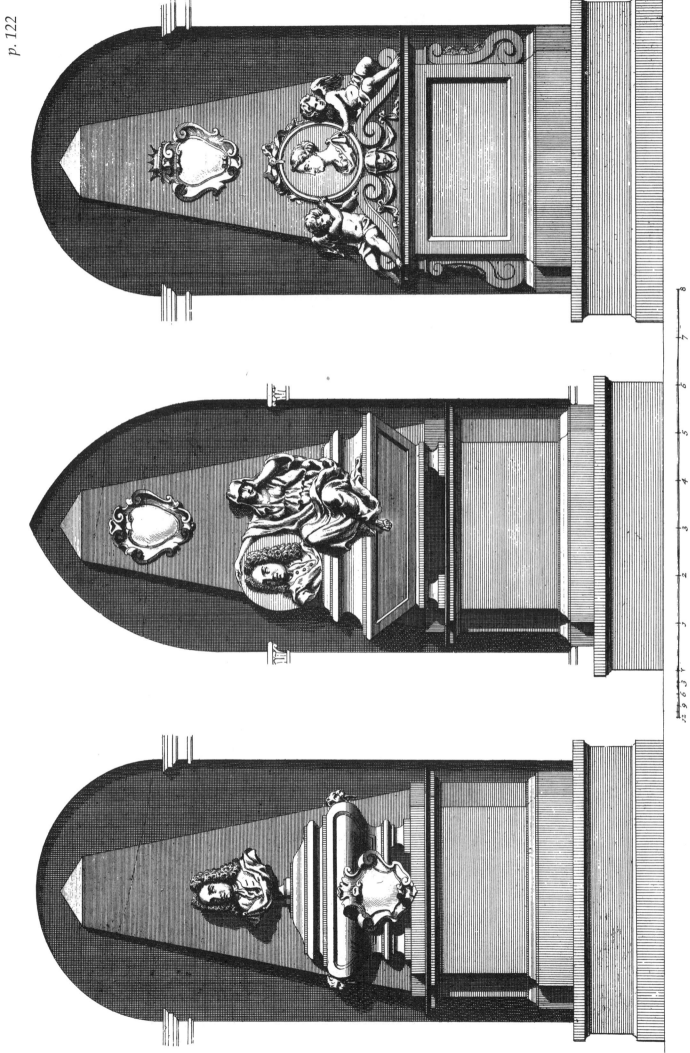

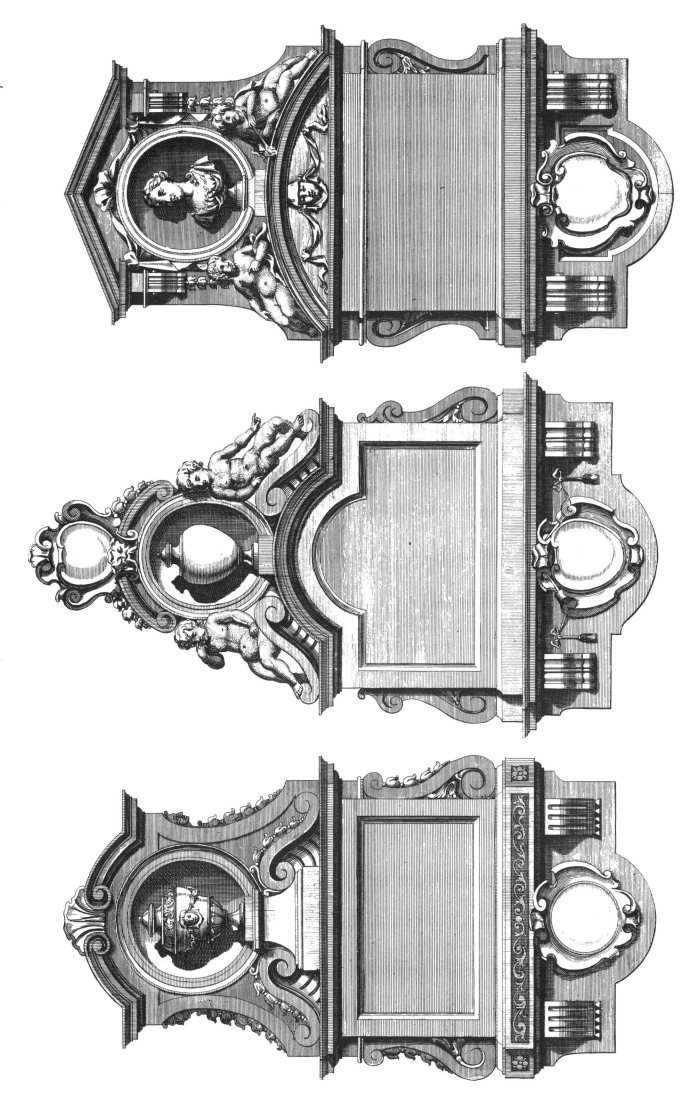

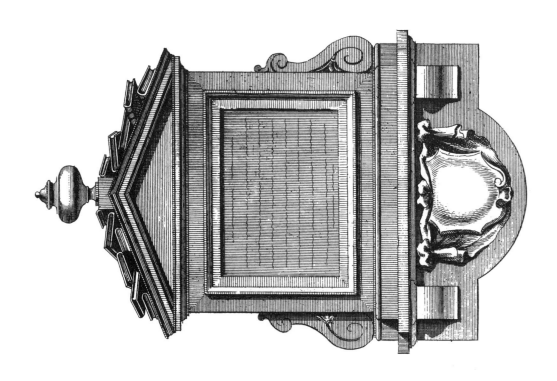

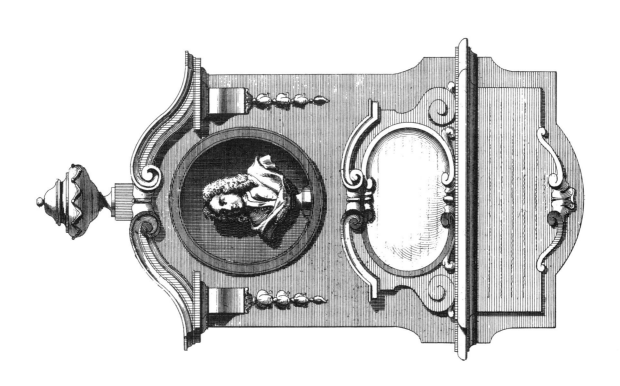

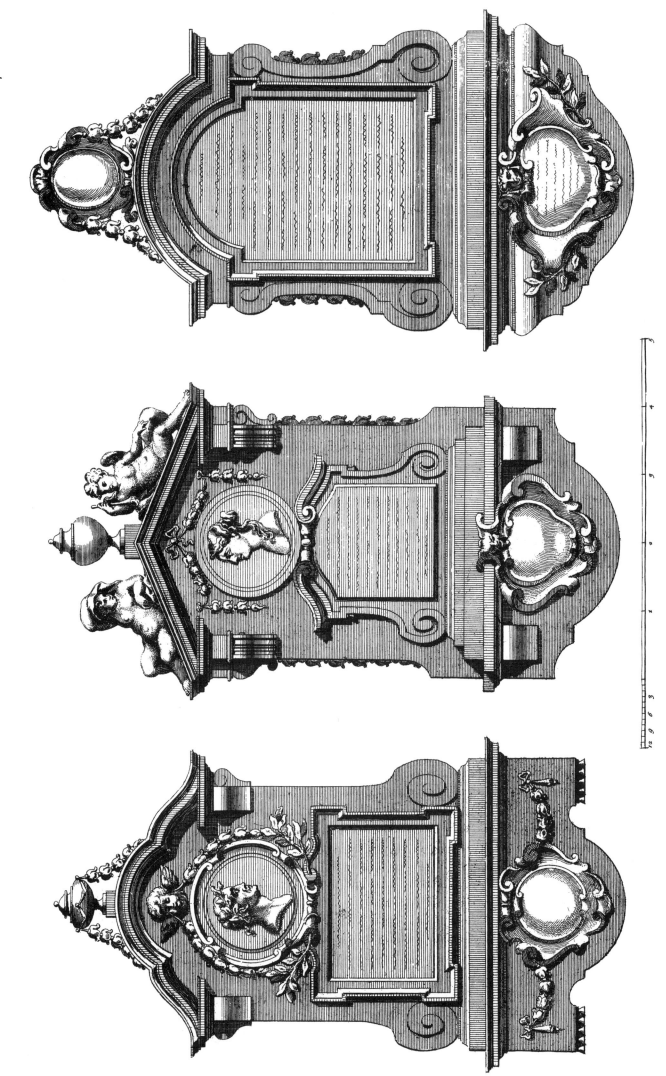

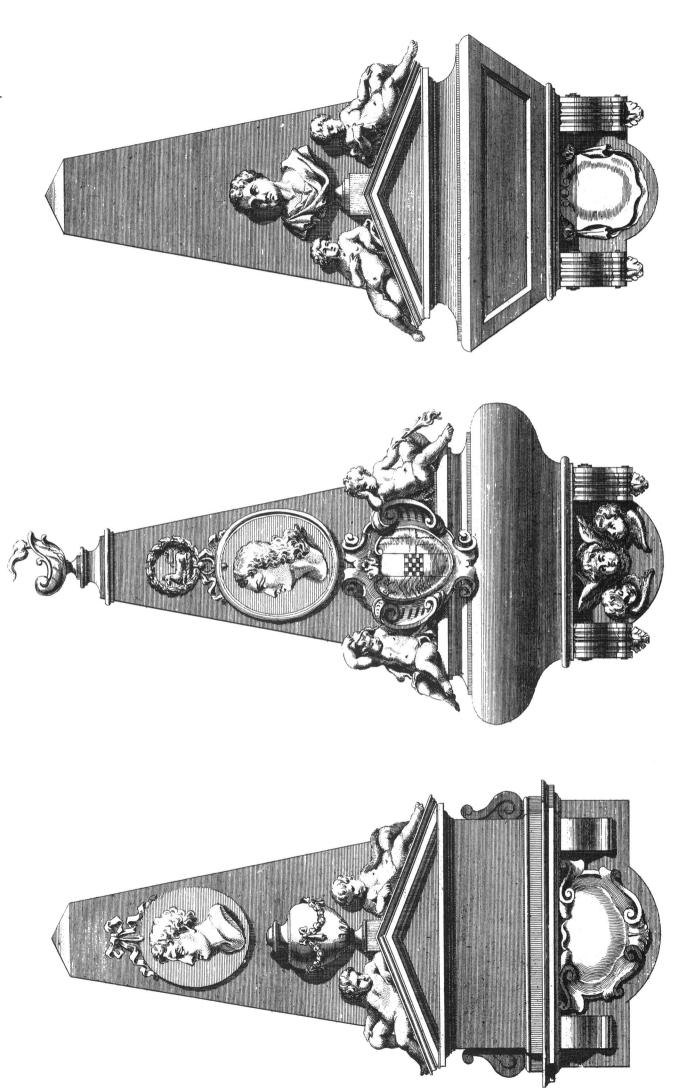

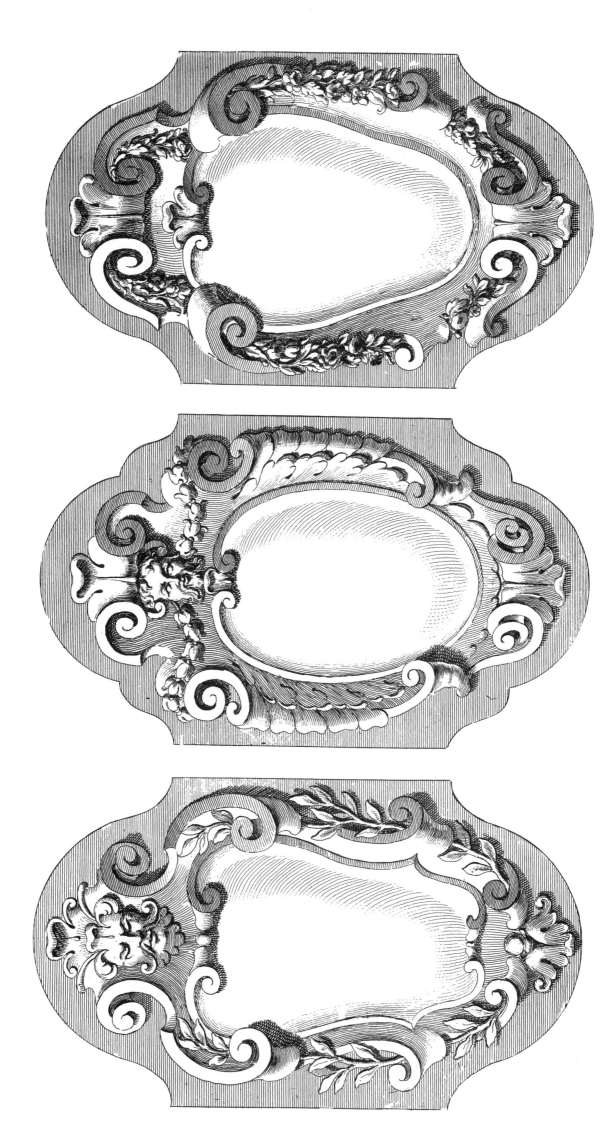

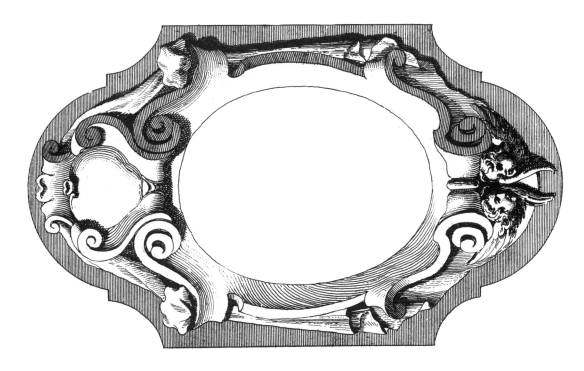

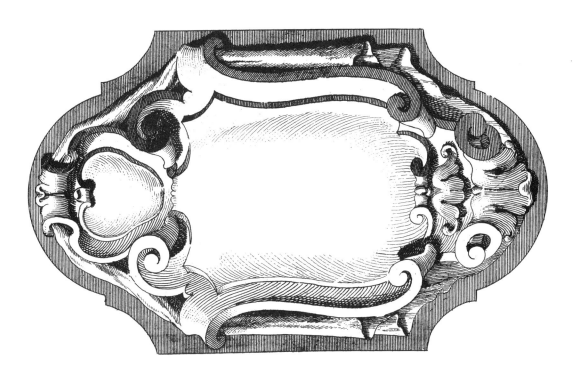

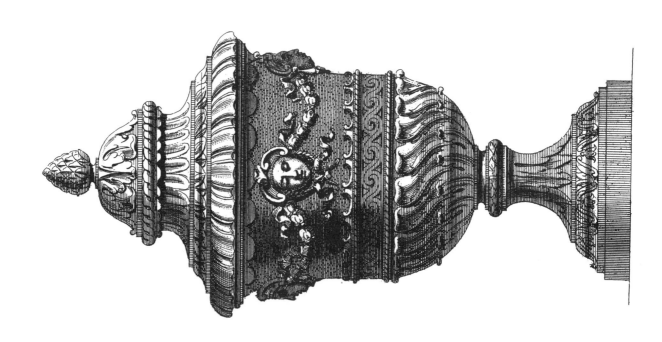

p. 142

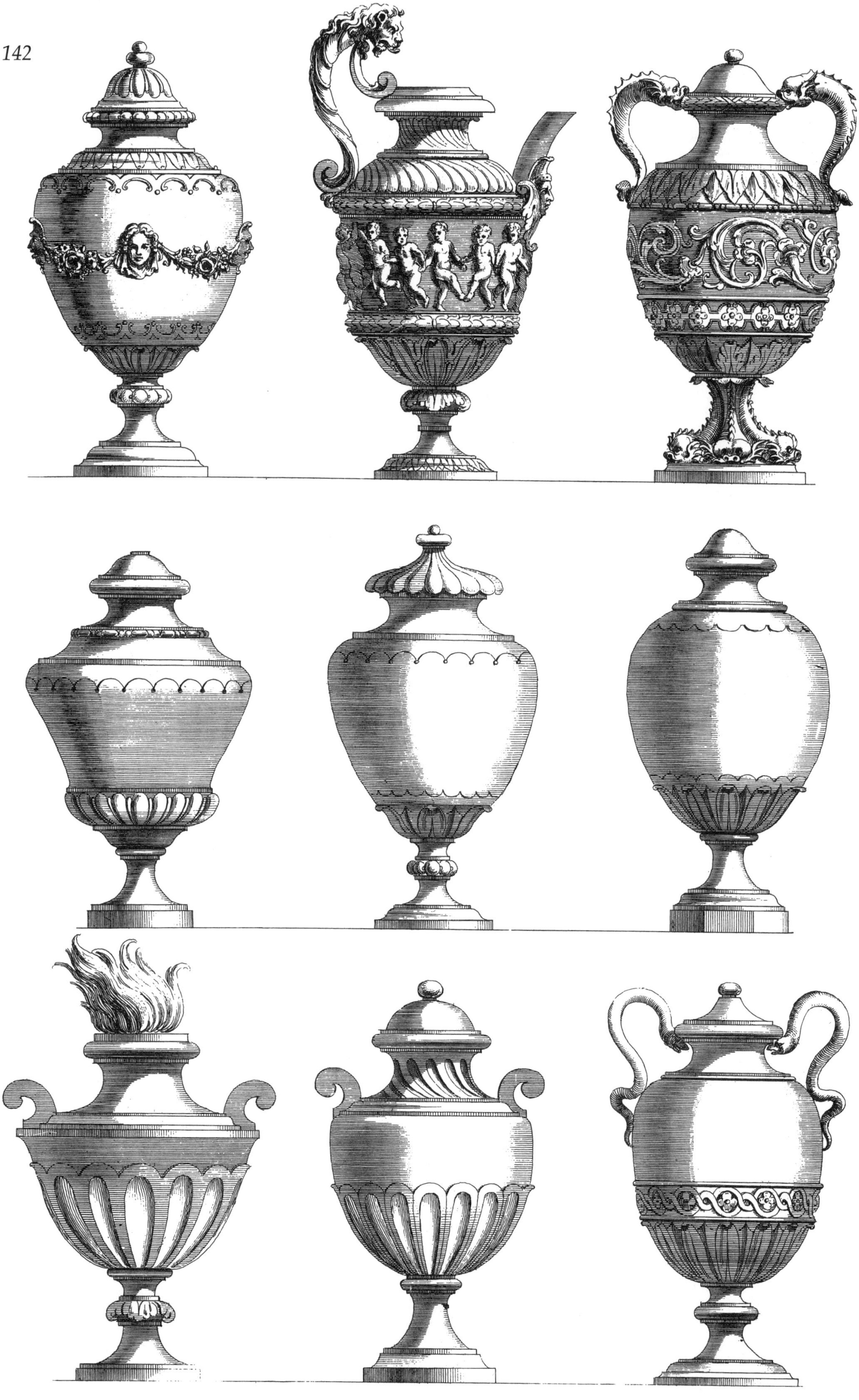

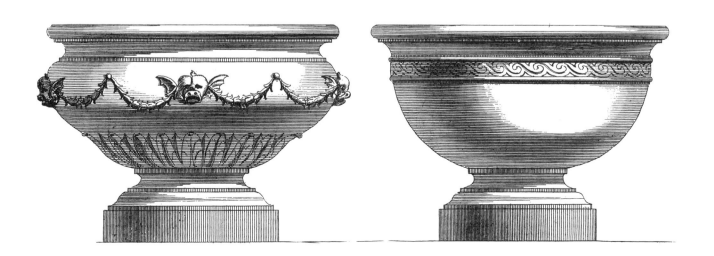

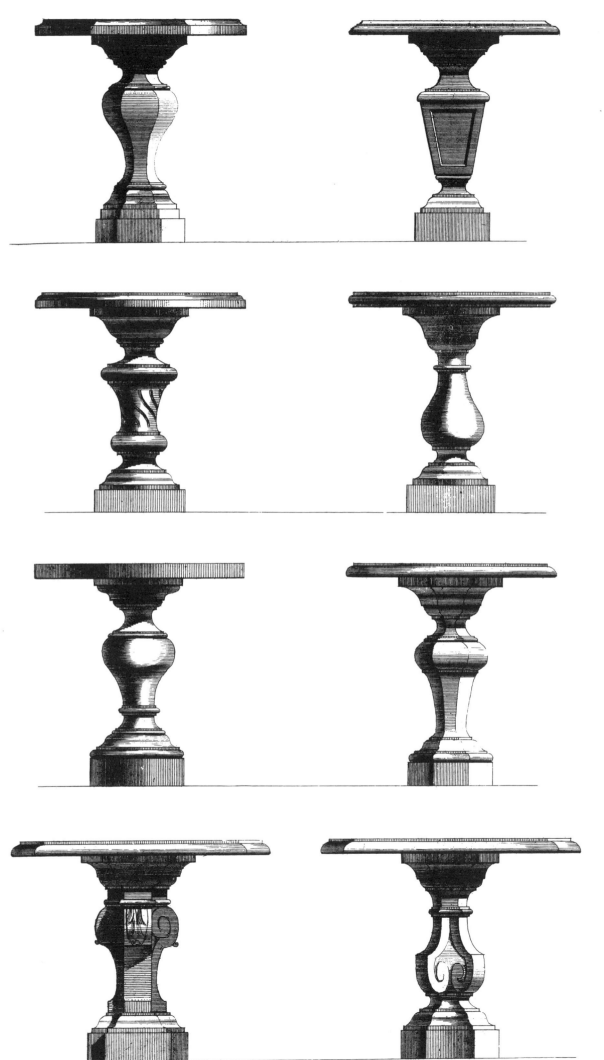

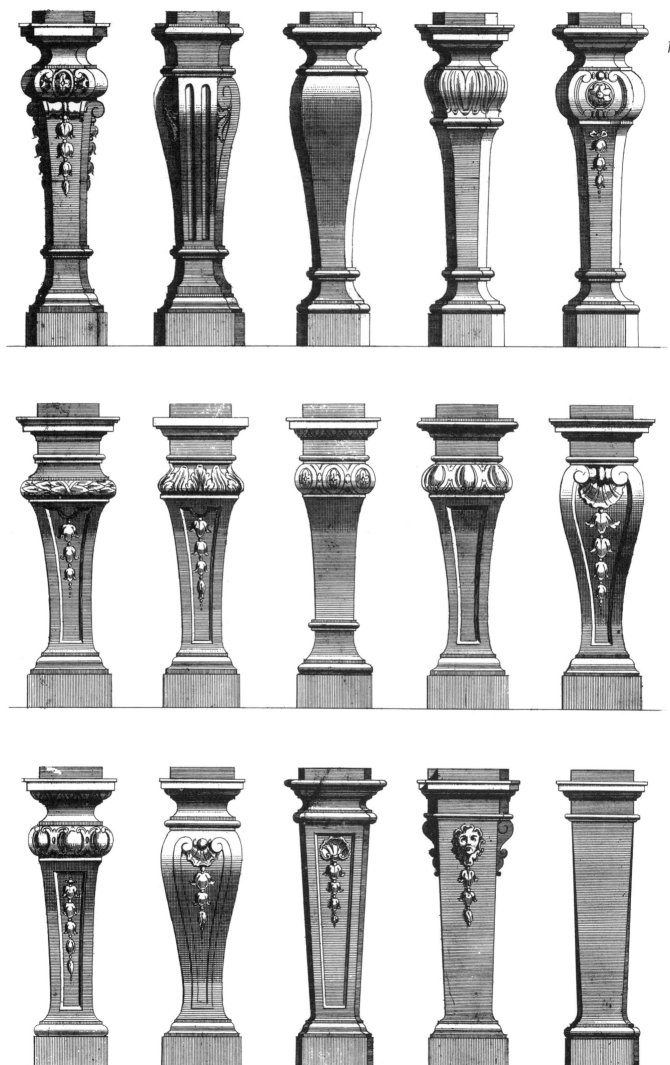